# F4F WILDCAT VS A6M2-N "RUFE"

## Solomon Islands 1942–43

MICHAEL JOHN CLARINGBOULD

OSPREY
Bloomsbury Publishing Plc
Kemp House, Chawley Park, Cumnor Hill, Oxford, OX2 9PH, UK
Bloomsbury Publishing Ireland Limited,
29 Earlsfort Terrace, Dublin 2, D02 AY28, Ireland
Bloomsbury Publishing Inc.
1359 Broadway, 12th Floor, New York, NY 10018, USA
E-mail: info@ospreypublishing.com

OSPREY is a trademark of Osprey Publishing Ltd

First published in Great Britain in 2026



A catalogue record for this book is available from the British Library.

ISBN: PB: 9781472870742; eBook 9781472870759; ePDF 9781472870728; XML 9781472870735

26 27 28 29 30 10 9 8 7 6 5 4 3 2 1

Edited by Tony Holmes
Cover artwork and battlescene by Gareth Hector
Three-views, cockpit views, and armament views by Jim Laurier
Maps by www.bounford.com
Index by Alan Rutter
Typeset by Lumina Datamatics Ltd
Printed by Repro India Ltd

MIX Paper
FSC FSC® C047271



**Acknowledgments**
Considerable thanks are extended to French author Bernard Baeza for sharing his knowledge and rare photographs. Thank you also to Pacific War Air Historical Associates members Ed DeKiep, Luca Ruffato (deceased), Osamu Tagaya, and Jim Lansdale (deceased). Finally, thanks to Ryan Toews for IJNAF markings collaboration and technical expertise, Russell Harada (of Lae, Papua New Guinea) for his assistance with the translation of archaic kanji script, and Yumi Ezaki in Canberra for assisting with the translation of Adm Jinichi Kusaka's diary.

**F4F-4 Wildcat cover artwork**
On November 7, 1942, 802nd Kokutai buntaicho Lt Hideo Goto led five of the unit's A6M2-N Sui-sen, with another from *Kamikawa Maru* and two F1M2 "Petes," to cover an incoming destroyer supply run to Guadalcanal. Headed for the same convoy, and flying top cover, were eight F4F-4 Wildcats from VMF-121 (led by Capt Joe Foss) and an identical number from VMF-112 (led by Maj Paul Fontana). They were accompanying eight USAAF P-39 Airacobras armed with 500-lb bombs that had become separated en route by mixed weather conditions – clouds interspersed with bands of rain.

Just north of Vangunu Island, about 150 miles northwest of Henderson Field, on Guadalcanal, the floatplane formation detoured to attack a solitary SBD Dauntless returning home from conducting a reconnaissance patrol. It was then that Foss spotted the IJNAF floatplanes below them, and seized the opportunity to make a "hit and run" attack. The first pass and subsequent combat was decisive, with all six Sui-sen being shot down. Amongst five pilots lost by 802nd Kokutai was FPO2c Hisao Jitou in W-107, and this aircraft is depicted here in artwork being engaged in a head-on pass by an F4F-4 from VMF-121. (Cover artwork by Gareth Hector)

**A6M2-N "Rufe" cover artwork**
At dawn of October 30, 1942, a combined formation of seven VMO-251 and VMF-212 F4F-3/4 Wildcats led by 1Lt Jack Conger (of the latter unit) arrived overhead the Japanese seaplane base at Rekata Bay just before sunrise. Hoping to surprise their IJNAF foes, they had been guided to the target by lit kerosene lamps scattered throughout the Japanese camp. Activity at the base had started early that morning to prepare a combined formation of 12 floatplanes to escort the IJN destroyers *Shigure* and *Ariake* returning to Tonolei Harbor following an overnight supply run to Guadalcanal. The planned patrol was for three 14th Kokutai Sui-sen, along with one from *Kamikawa Maru*, to accompany eight F1M3 "Petes." The aircraft had flown in to Rekata Bay from the Shortland Islands the previous afternoon, and their arrival had been reported by a Coastwatcher to American forces on Guadalcanal.

Their approach masked by poor visibility due to low cloud, the Wildcat pilots reached their target just as the Sui-sen were departing. Mission leader Lt Hideo Goto had just gotten airborne when the Wildcats hit him during the critical take-off phase. Nevertheless, Hideo managed to climb away. The following three Sui-sen pilots persisted with their take-off runs, and a second flight of Wildcats hit Superior Flyer Teruo Watanabe's floatplane fighter. It broke apart when the aircraft hit the water, although a shaken Teruo survived. Goto, meanwhile, aborted plans to cover the convoy and headed for the Shortland Islands instead, where his badly-damaged Sui-sen was written off. The two remaining Sui-sen pilots, FPO1c Eiji Matsuyama (in W-107) and FCPO Hisao Jitou, briefly fought the Wildcats before also disappearing toward the Shortlands in the mist. The main float on Jitou's floatplane was badly sieved by the Wildcat attack, causing the Sui-sen to sink in shallow water when it arrived at the Shortlands. This airframe was written off also. (Cover artwork by Gareth Hector)

**Previous Page**
US Marine Corps Wildcat aces Maj John Smith, 2Lt Ken Frazier and Majs John Dobbin and Robert Galer at Henderson Field in October 1942. Although these pilots claimed 52 victories between them, Smith was the only one to be credited with the downing of a "float Zero" (on October 10, 1942). (Author's Collection)

# CONTENTS

# INTRODUCTION

The numerous aerial battles which unfolded overhead Bougainville, Guadalcanal, and the Solomon Islands throughout 1942 and into 1943 were studded by scattered yet unique confrontations between Imperial Japanese Naval Air Force (IJNAF) floatplanes and Allied land-based fighters. It was during such encounters that F4F-4 Wildcat pilots sometimes came across the A6M2-N Sui-sen fighter, which they termed "float Zeros," "single-float fighters," or "Zeros on Floats." The aircraft was later allocated the

Four F1M2 "Petes" from *Kunikawa Maru*, three 802nd Kokutai Sui-sen, and a solitary E13A1 "Jake" moored in the shallows off Poporang Island in early 1943. (Author's Collection)

Allied reporting name "Rufe." The special breed of Japanese pilots flying these aircraft made such an impression on their enemy in combat through a combination of maneuverability and tenacity that their Sui-sen were often misidentified as conventional Zero-sen fighters.

To date, the combat presence of the Sui-sen in the South Pacific theater has been both opaque and attended by inaccurate attention. Nonetheless, the clashes between the Sui-sen and F4F-4 Wildcat in 1942–43 offer instructive and comparative insight into the limitations and eccentricities of air power in such a widespread tropical theater.

Although the first detachment of Sui-sen to the South Seas was wiped out by strafing Wildcats during the August 7, 1942 Guadalcanal invasion, the inventory in the Solomons was quickly bolstered via the arrival of the seaplane tender *Kamikawa Maru* exactly four weeks later. A series of intense air battles saw these aircraft in turn decimated by mid-November. However, in the interim, another Sui-sen unit, 14th Kokutai, also took up station in the Shortland Islands on October 12. This unit, which became 802nd Kokutai on November 1, 1942 during an IJNAF restructure, fought on until March 1943, when it was withdrawn to another theater. In nearly eight months of persistent combat in the Solomons, and when they were not attacking US Army Air Forces (USAAF) B-17E Flying Fortresses, the Sui-sens' most persistent adversary remained the sturdy F4F-4 Wildcat.

Like their land-based brethren, IJNAF floatplane fighter pilots lacked an adequate early-warning system, leading to insufficient time to intercept intruders – this was not the case for their Wildcat counterparts flying from Guadalcanal. Instead, Sui-sen pilots were forced to engage in lengthy, often pointless, standing patrols overhead their

Capt Joe Foss's VMF-121 division of eight pilots (seven of whom can be seen here) called themselves "Joe's Flying Circus" while flying from Guadalcanal in late 1942. These men are, from left to right, 1Lt Greg Loesch, 2Lts Oscar Bate and 2Lt Frank Presley, Capt Joe Foss, and 2Lts Roger Haberman, Tom Furlow, and Bill Freeman. Foss was almost certainly the only one of these pilots to claim a "float Zero" victory (on November 7, 1942). (Author's Collection)

Shortlands base. If not already airborne when an Allied air attack occurred, they usually scrambled too late, leaving them to be either attacked at a disadvantage, or finding themselves vainly climbing in pursuit of enemy aircraft already well on their way home.

Supplying replacement Sui-sen to the South Pacific theater proved to be a challenge for the IJNAF, which also struggled with the provision of pilots after the initial cadre, who, in some cases, were better trained than their US counterparts, was lost in combat. The limited number of serviceable Sui-sen at forward bases prevented newly-arrived pilots from accruing much-needed experience. In the first months of their South Pacific war, 'green' pilots fresh from flying training in Japan were only gradually immersed into combat led by veterans. Typically, they only flew benign and often extended patrols, or even conducted training exercises instead. Nevertheless, during such activities, they sometimes had unexpected encounters with enemy aircraft, leading to losses.

Wildcat pilots new to the theater quickly worked out that the best way to escape the attentions of a well flown, maneuverable Sui-sen – routinely confused with a Zero-sen – was to dive and accelerate away. This tactic proved to be both sound and sensible, saving lives and enabling pilots to fight another day. More experienced aviators often chose to engage Sui-sen directly, although the Allied maxim of the time, "Never dogfight a Zero," was fittingly impressed upon Wildcat pilots, at least when they first arrived in-theater. The tactic of choice against any maneuverable Japanese fighter was a single high-speed pass, preferably from above – a tactic which applied against the Sui-sen as well.

Floatplane fighters had the advantage of operating from Rekata Bay (named by the Japanese as Re-ka-ta in Katakana), on Santa Isabel Island, which was close to Allied facilities and especially the vitally important Henderson Field on Guadalcanal. They chose to use this location on their own terms, minimizing their exposure to Allied air attack by routinely evacuating the base and heading back to the Shortlands to avoid such raids. Nonetheless, sometimes they were caught out when the pressure of providing air cover meant that they stayed longer at Rekata Bay than the pilots would have preferred.

This somewhat elusive capability of the Sui-sen made for several curious encounters with Wildcats, including conducting a daring surprise raid against Guadalcanal. The impact of these battles on the overall South Pacific air war was, in reality, insignificant. However, the deployment of this unique floatplane fighter against the F4F-4 resulted in a series of fascinating encounters being fought out in a remote and hostile tropical theater.

# CHRONOLOGY

**1935**

| | |
|---|---|
| August | US Navy's Bureau of Aeronautics initiates a design competition for a new carrier fighter. |

**1936**

| | |
|---|---|
| March | US Navy awards a contract to Grumman for one XF4F-1 carrier-based biplane fighter. |
| July | US Navy places a contract for a completely revised Grumman design as the XF4F-2 monoplane fighter. |

**1937**

| | |
|---|---|
| May | Imperial Japanese Navy (IJN) issues preliminary planning document for the Prototype 12-Shi Carrier-based fighter, intended as a replacement for the A5M Type 96 Carrier Fighter. |

**1938**

| | |
|---|---|
| October | US Navy awards Grumman a contract for the improved XF4F-3 carrier fighter. |

**1939**

| | |
|---|---|
| February 12 | XF4F-3 makes its first flight. |
| April 1 | Mitsubishi Prototype 12-Shi Carrier Fighter makes its first flight. |
| August | US Navy awards contract for Grumman to build 54 F4F-3 Wildcats. |

**1940**

| | |
|---|---|
| February | First flight of a production F4F-3. |
| September | IJN Headquarters issues specification 15-Shi for a floatplane fighter, which will be closely based on the 12-Shi Carrier Fighter. |
| December | Deliveries of the F4F-3 commence, with US Navy fighter squadrons VF-4 and VF-7 receiving the first examples. |

**1941**

| | |
|---|---|
| April 14 | XF4F-4 makes its first flight. |
| December 7 | IJNAF carrier-based aircraft attack the Pacific Fleet at Pearl Harbor. |
| December 8 | The interim A6M2-N Sui-sen makes its maiden flight in Japan. |

**1942**

| | |
|---|---|
| April 1 | Yokohama Kokutai is created in Japan, becoming the first combat unit to deploy operationally with the A6M2-N Sui-sen. |
| May 2 | IJNAF floatplanes use Rekata Bay for the first time when Nakajima E8N "Dave" and Mitsubishi F1M "Pete" floatplanes from *Kamikawa Maru* participate in the unsuccessful Operation *MO* (attack on Port Moresby). |
| June 10 | Sui-sen conducts its first aerial combat when five attempt unsuccessfully to intercept USAAF B-26 Marauders retreating from an attack against Rabaul. |
| July 5 | Yokohama Kokutai Sui-sen conduct their first patrol from Tulagi/Halavo Bay. |
| July 17 | Yokohama Kokutai pilot FPO1c Tatsuo Hori is shot down and killed during an encounter with a lone 435th Bombardment Squadron (BS) B-17E, marking the first Sui-sen lost in combat. |
| August 7 | US Marine Corps invades Guadalcanal and Tulagi. In a strafing attack on Florida and Tanambago Islands, F4F-4s from VF-71 destroy the entire Yokohama Kokutai (ten A6M2-Ns and seven H6K4 "Mavis" flying boats), bar two/three Sui-sen away visiting the Shortlands. |

| | |
|---|---|
| August 20 | VMF-223 is transferred to Guadalcanal (Henderson Field) with 19 F4F-4s. |
| August 28 | R-Area Force is established by the IJN in response to the August 7 landings. The Force's operational component is 11th Seaplane Tender Division. |
| September 4 | *Kamikawa Maru* delivers 11 Sui-sen to the Shortlands. |
| September 5 | Seaplane tender *Akitsushima* significantly reinforces Rekata Bay, adding considerable refueling capacity and enabling IJNAF floatplanes to strike Henderson Field. |
| September 14 | Eleven VF-5 Wildcats engage four Sui-sen near Henderson Field and down three. This is the first air-to-air combat between the two types. |
| October 4 | Following months of intense combat, the R-Area Force inventory stands at 12 F1M2 "Petes," five *Kamikawa Maru* Sui-sen, and nine Aichi E13A1 "Jakes" from the *Chitose* and *Sanyo Maru* detachments. |
| October 12 | Nine Sui-sen fly down to Poporang Island, in the Solomons, from Rabaul, having been delivered to the theater by *Kiyokawa Maru*. |
| November 1 | R-Area Force is restructured, with 14th Kokutai being redesignated 802nd Kokutai. |
| November 7 | The modest Sui-sen force suffers its largest single loss in aerial combat in the South Pacific when six are shot down, along with one F1M2 "Pete." They are intercepted during a late afternoon destroyer patrol by F4F-4s from VMF-121 and VMF-112 and USAAF Airacobras. |
| December | Ballale Island and Munda airfields become operational for the IJNAF. |
| December 17 | In Japan, a rejuvenated 802nd Kokutai is allocated 15 Sui-sen, with 16 additional pilots. They depart Yokosuka on January 2, 1943 aboard *Kunikawa Maru*, with the initial six Sui-sen bound for Poporang Island. The remaining nine are later delivered to Rabaul aboard merchantman in separate batches. |

## 1943

| | |
|---|---|
| February 12 | The first F4U Corsairs arrive at Guadalcanal, the new fighters eventually replacing the F4F-4s. |
| February 13 | The last Sui-sen combat victory is credited to Lt Keizou Yamazaki, who mistakenly claims a P-39 instead of the P-40 he was actually fighting. |
| February 14 | The "Saint Valentine's Day Massacre" sees American units lose nine aircraft over south Bougainville against only one Japanese loss. The debacle showcases IJNAF fighter tactics, including the potency of the Sui-sen in combat. A pause in combat over Bougainville ensues while the Americans reconsider their tactics. |
| March 13 | 802nd Kokutai's 13 remaining Sui-sen redeploy to Jaluit, in the Marshall Islands, this operation marking the last Sui-sen flight in the South Seas theater. |
| April 15 | All surviving floatplanes of the depleted R-Area Force are amalgamated into a new unit, 938th Kokutai. |
| August | IJNAF seaplanes use Rekata Bay for the last time. |

# DESIGN AND DEVELOPMENT

## GRUMMAN F4F-4 WILDCAT

The prototype XF4F-2 from which the production F4F-3 Wildcat derived was an all-metal monoplane with stressed-skin and a single main wing spar. The outer wing sections were bolted to the fuselage center section. Pneumatically-operated flaps were quick to deploy and proved efficient. The ancillary surfaces of rudder, ailerons, and elevators were fabric and dope-covered. Two Plexiglas windows in the fuselage just

Seven brand new F4F-4s fresh off the production line have been posed to show the benefit of the Grumman-patented "Sto-wing." The rearwards-folding wing was designed by the company and so successfully trialed on the F4F-4 that it was incorporated into later Grumman-designed carrier-based aircraft. (Public Domain)

**OPPOSITE PAGE**
F4F-4 BuNo 03508 was the second Wildcat most often flown by VMF-223 pilot, and high-scoring ace, Capt Marion Carl – both examples bore the squadron number "black 13." Carl scored 12 victories in his first "black 13," BuNo 02100, prior to being shot down in it at midday on September 9, 1942 during a high-altitude combat at 22,000ft with a Tainan Kokutai Zero-sen. Flying his 13th mission from Henderson Field at the time, he parachuted into the ocean offshore Guadalcanal. With the assistance of villagers, he was returned to his unit four days later. Not one for superstition, Carl selected replacement F4F-4 BuNo 03508, which he also numbered "black 13." On September 27 Carl claimed one and one shared G4M1 "Betty" bombers destroyed in this Wildcat, followed by a Zero-sen on October 3. BuNo 03508 was recycled through a maintenance unit and then transferred to VMF-223's sister-squadron VMF-224 in early November 1942. It was written off with this unit on the 11th of that same month following an operational accident at Henderson Field.

beneath the forward wing afforded the pilot limited downward azimuth visibility. Both main gears retracted flush into the fuselage, activated by turning the gear handle some 30 revolutions, which rotated a worm gear.

The F4F-3, the first production model of the Wildcat, was fitted with the Pratt & Whitney R-1830-76 engine, with improved -86 and -90 models installed in the later F4F-4. Ultimately, Grumman delivered 185 F4F-3s (without self-sealing fuel tanks and only limited armor protection) to the US Navy and US Marine Corps. A comprehensive redesign of the F4F-3 resulted in development of the F4F-4, and by the end of 1942 Grumman had delivered 1,169 examples of the latter aircraft to the US Navy and US Marine Corps. Built to withstand repeated carrier landings, the design of the Wildcat resulted in a truly robust airframe.

The improved F4F-4 featured folding wings of a unique design, more powerful armament, and comprehensive armor plating. The folding wing (patented by Grumman as the "Sto-wing") was developed after the US Navy expressed a desire to embark more fighters on a carrier. In March 1940, the company developed a folding-wing mechanism and installed it in an F4F-3. Legend has it that Grumman engineers worked out the concept using a rubber eraser and paper clips. The folding-wing section, attached to two stubs connected to the fuselage, allowed the outer wings to be pivoted back against the fuselage, thus reducing the span from 38ft to a little over 14ft. As the XF4F-4, the prototype made its first flight on April 14, 1941. Initially, the folding-wing mechanism was hydraulic, but to save weight this system was removed and the wings folded manually.

By the late 1930s, both the US Navy and the USAAC had determined that the 0.30-cal. machine gun installed in its fighters was too ineffectual against all-metal airframes, many furnished with armor and self-sealing fuel tanks. While cannon were also considered, the Browning M2 0.50-cal. machine gun seemed the best compromise,

Re-arming an F4F-3A on board USS *Enterprise* (CV-6) during February–March 1942. The fixed wings and gun barrels for two of the four 0.50-cal. M2s synonymous with this variant are clearly visible. (National Archives and Records Administration (NARA))

# F4F-4 WILDCAT

New six-gun and "Sto-wing" F4F-4s of VF-6 on the deck of *Enterprise* shortly before the Battle of Midway in June 1942. By the end of the previous month, all three Wildcat squadrons assigned to Pacific Fleet carriers had been re-equipped with the F4F-4 – some 27 aircraft could be embarked thanks to the advent of the "Sto-wing." (NARA)

offering a firm rate of fire and a high muzzle velocity. These factors gave it the necessary range and power to be an effective aerial weapon.

Compared with the four-gun F4F-3, each F4F-4 added an extra 0.50-cal. weapon to the outboard wing, fed with 240 rounds of ammunition per gun. However, this increase in firepower came at the expense of reduced ammunition holdings per gun. Many Wildcat pilots retained the strong opinion that the F4F-3's original configuration of four 0.50-cal. machine guns was more suited to aerial combat, as it gave greater weapons endurance. Furthermore, after experiencing combat with Japanese aircraft, Naval Aviators felt that four 0.50-cal. machine guns were perfectly adequate for dealing with the less-ruggedly constructed Zero-sen and other IJNAF types.

For the purposes of combating the Zero-sen or Sui-sen, the heavier F4F-4 was less maneuverable than the F4F-3 too. This additional weight was courtesy of 150lb of armor for the oil tank and behind the pilot's seat, a 27lb bullet-resistant windscreen replacing the earlier standard glass windscreen, and self-sealing fuel tanks. These additional components added about 900 lbs to the Wildcat's gross weight, commensurately reducing the maximum speed from 331mph in the F4F-3 to 318mph in the F4F-4. More significantly for Guadalcanal operations, the extra weight reduced the rate-of-climb from 2,300ft down to 2,190ft per minute.

The first F4F-4s were assigned to VF-71 on board USS *Wasp* (CV-7) in February 1942, followed by VF-8 on board USS *Hornet* (CV-8), both carriers then serving with the Atlantic Fleet. By the end of May 1942, most of the US Navy's fighter squadrons, and two US Marine Corps units, had converted to the F4F-4. Indeed, it was the most ubiquitous of all models which fought from Guadalcanal throughout 1942–43 – the only F4F-3s to see action from the island were a small number assigned to VMO-251 for most of its initial deployment to Henderson Field.

# NAKAJIMA A6M2-N SUI-SEN

The Nakajima A6M2-N Type 2 Sui-sen was essentially a modified A6M2 Zero-sen, which aircraft designer Jiro Horikoshi created to meet the strategic demands of the air war over China. In 1942, the Zero-sen represented cutting-edge technology, and even though designed as a carrier-based fighter, it proved instantly adaptable to land-based operations in the South Pacific. The A6M was the IJNAF's most ubiquitous fighter in South Pacific skies, and from the outset the aircraft gained a reputation for being a dependable warhorse. The type's 950hp Nakajima Sakae 12 engine with a single-stage supercharger was especially reliable, enabling the fighter to patrol at 20,000ft with ease and climb as high as 30,000ft if required.

While the first Zero-sen were undergoing trial by combat in China, Japan's IJN Headquarters issued specification 15-Shi for a floatplane fighter in September 1940. The concept was that such a fighter could be based off small islands or in sheltered bays where airfields could not be built. Ultimately, Japan would in fact become the only nation to deploy floatplane fighters during World War II. The design contract was awarded to Kawanishi, which designated the type the N1K1. Ambitiously, it incorporated contra-rotating propellers, which in turn presented a suite of inherent technical challenges that proved hard to resolve. IJNAF impatience was sidelined by turning to developing an existing airframe type as an interim measure while Kawanishi became increasingly engrossed in resolving a growing list of powerplant problems.

The A6M2, a proven and successful fighter, offered the best platform for an interim design, and a contract for the modification work was awarded to Nakajima. While the company already had manufacturing drawings for the Zero-sen from Mitsubishi in its possession, undertaking airframe modifications from plans alone was considered too complicated a task. Instead, a damaged A6M2 that had been sent to Nakajima for repair was removed from the workshop then reconfigured as the first test bed. All modifications to 15-Shi specification were undertaken on this airframe, and when completed it became the prototype Sui-sen.

Nakajima's obvious and main challenge was to add floats, hopefully without compromising the exceptional manoeuvrability that characterized the A6M2. Within Nakajima, the project became known as the AS-1, with Chief Engineer Shinobu Mitake in charge of the conversion. He had previously been involved in developing the IJNAF's E4N shipboard reconnaissance floatplane of the early 1930s, the Experimental 12-shi fighter, and the E8N2 reconnaissance floatplane, later given the Allied reporting name "Dave."

Mitake considered that a single main pylon – into

An early-build (possibly even one of two prototypes built by Nakajima) A6M2-N is seen on a slipway at Lake Kasumigaura in late 1942/early 1943. The small ventral fin beneath the tail, added to offer extra stability in flight, and the trailing rudder on the main float can both be seen here. (Public Domain)

**OPPOSITE PAGE**

On December 17, 1942 in Yokosuka, Lt Cdr Tsunemaru Eto, formerly the *Kamikawa Maru* hikotaicho, was appointed to head a rejuvenated 802 Kokutai. Fifteen Sui-sen, with tail codes N1-101 to -115, and 16 pilots, led by buntaicho Lt(jg) Takeo Yokoyama, were assigned to the unit. The pilots departed Yokosuka on January 2, 1943 aboard *Kunikawa Maru* with six of the new floatplanes, along with 12 new F1M2 "Petes" destined for 958th Kokutai. A further nine Sui-sen for 802nd Kokutai followed aboard several merchantmen, including this example, N1-112. Once in-theater, Buntaicho Yokoyama and his incoming replacement pilots were delivered to Poporang by H6K4 "Mavis" flying boat on January 15, 1943. N1-112 was photographed at Poporang the following month, just prior to the unit's redeployment to Jaluit. Unusually, the airframe received a field-applied green camouflage scheme at Poporang shortly before departing the theater, although the top half of the fin featuring the tail code and unit marking was left in its original Nakajima factory color. Note the small red star representing one aerial victory on the top half of the rudder above the numerals "112."

which the A6M2's oil cooler air intake could be housed – offered the best aerodynamic solution. The Zero-sen's wheel wells were not faired over, as is so often and wrongly claimed, the floatplane's wing omitting the undercarriage wells completely. This duly meant that it was stronger than the original A6M2 wing. Carry-through stringers were fitted in the former wheel wells, and all undercarriage attachment points and housings were removed. In addition, the Sui-sen's engine mounts and bushings were made structurally stronger than those for the Sakae 12 in the A6M2. These modifications were made so that the Sui-sen could withstand water-borne flight operations in rough seas, as these placed considerable and additional strains on the airframe not replicated by land-based operations.

Following the prototype's first flight on December 8, 1941 at Lake Kasumigaura, it was determined that the Sui-sen settled too quickly when landing. This characteristic was resolved by increasing flap availability on final approach. Tight taxiing turns on the water in high winds also proved challenging, even with bursts of additional engine power, due to the aircraft's modest-sized rudder. The latter was, in fact, larger than the example fitted to the A6M2 in order to compensate for yaw induced by the large float when airborne, Nakajima having incorporated a small ventral fin under the main one to offer extra stability in flight. This problem was resolved by installing a trailing submerged rudder on the main float.

The simple modifications to improve the floatplane's handling characteristics on the water were made to the prototype the same afternoon the aircraft had completed its maiden flight.

A second prototype was delivered on February 9, 1942 for strength tests, with the latter seeing the airframe hoisted to different heights and then dropped into a test tank. Nakajima engineer Atsushi Tajima supervised these tests, during which the main pylon attaching the main float to the fuselage unexpectedly buckled via compression. Robust discussions ensued between engineers as to whether it had collapsed due to a design flaw, defective materials, or poor welding. The matter was settled when stronger welds compellingly resolved the issue.

Further airframe issues arose on the second prototype in March 1942 when it was discovered that several magnesium alloy parts had badly corroded due to electrolysis. These parts included underside wing access panels, numerous other fuselage access hatches and covers, and structural fittings across the main float. All were replaced with duralumin. Five more pre-production Sui-sen had been delivered to Nakajima for further tests by the end of March 1942, upon which a suite of minor modifications were made.

The main float incorporated an auxiliary 330-liter fuel tank, equipped with a fuel purge system that was adapted from the Walter-Kidde mechanism installed in pre-war US Navy seaplanes. This enabled the pilot, in cases of emergency, to jettison the tank's fuel. In early-build Sui-sen models this system was covered under a bulbous housing. All these early batches of aircraft left the factory with a fuselage hinomaru lacking a white surround. The white "piping" was added to aircraft at the Nakajima factory from the end of August 1942, by which time the first 58 A6M2-Ns had been manufactured. As with the A6M2 Zero-sen, Nakajima painted interior parts of the airframe with aotake primer. However, it applied a special aluminum protective paint to the interior of the Sui-sen's flaps to ward off salt water corrosion.

A6M2-N SUI-SEN
28ft 8in.
N-112
10ft 0in.
39ft 4.7in.

The engine of Sui-sen YII-104 is warmed up during *Kamikawa Maru*'s return voyage to the South Seas theater that saw it deliver 11 floatplane fighters to the Shortland Islands from Japan in September 1942. Note the deck tie-down straps over the main float and the protective bulbous housing covering the fuel purge system immediately aft of the main pylon. The first batch of Sui-sen completed by Nakajima housed a fuel purge system adapted from the US Navy's Walter-Kidde mechanism within this housing. It enabled pilots to jettison the entire 330 liters of fuel contained in the float's tank. (Author's Collection)

The main float's forward pylon was bolted centrally to the front wing spar, whereas the two smaller supporting rear V-struts were attached to the rear spar. All landing and winching loads and shocks were transferred through the rest of the airframe via the two wing spars. Impact loads were spread via reinforcing high-tensile extrusions. The Sui-sen also incorporated three retractable handholds and foot pegs on both sides of the fuselage, these being located in such a way that pilots could mount and dismount the cockpit without getting wet.

Remarkably, the first batch of early Sui-sen retained the folding wingtips of the A6M2. This became apparent when examination of captured airframes from Halavo and Tulagi showed that both the retractable latch system and wingtip hinge components were extant.

Production commenced in April 1942, and a total of 327 Sui-sen floatplane fighters had left the Nakajima factory at Koizumi by the time construction of the aircraft stopped in September 1943. The hybrid Zero-sen on floats was officially termed the Type 2 Fighter Seaplane (2 Shiki Suijoh Sentoh-ki), abbreviated to Sui-sen. Following its first appearances, the Allies allocated the type the codename "Rufe." As matters turned out, by the time the purpose-built N1K1 Kyofu (christened "Rex" by the Allies) entered production in July 1943, the nature of the war in the Pacific had changed significantly.

Seaplane tenders often served as mother ships to Sui-sen and also transported them as floatplane transports. During delivery voyages over long distances, engines were warmed at frequent intervals. The floatplanes were lowered for delivery to the sea surface by derrick. Ancillary control braces made of wood were fixed to ailerons, elevators, and rudders during such voyages, for it was vital to keep control surfaces locked so as to avoid them being damaged by strong winds.

One of the floatplane's deficiencies was its lack of self-sealing fuel tanks – a flaw in almost all Japanese aircraft of the period. This meant that one incendiary bullet could destroy a Sui-sen quickly and often spectacularly. On the plus side, the Nakajima Sakae 12 was relatively easy to service, and IJNAF engineers proved skilled at maintaining their mounts, hampered as they were by crude support facilities at forward bases such as Tulagi, the Shortland Islands and Rekata Bay.

Despite its massive main float pylon, the A6M2 N remained highly maneuverable, particularly at lower altitudes. Nevertheless, in combat, the Sui-sen's performance was about 20 percent less than its derivative, the A6M2. Such a drop was significant, and it was the principal reason why the type struggled in aerial combat with Allied fighters.

**PREVIOUS PAGE**
A rare inflight photograph of four recently delivered A6M2-Ns in close formation prior to being sent to the South Seas theater. Aircraft in both of the schemes seen here were flown in the Solomons in 1942–43. The size of the main float and its forward pylon are emphasized from this angle. (Public Domain)

**F4F-4 Wildcat and A6M2-N Sui-sen Comparison Specifications**

| | **F4F-4 Wildcat** | **A6M2-N** |
|---|---|---|
| Powerplant | 1,200hp Pratt & Whitney R-1830 | 950hp Nakajima Sakae 12 |
| **Dimensions** | | |
| Span | 38ft 0in. | 39ft 4.7in. |
| Length | 28ft 9in. | 33ft 2in. |
| Height | 11ft 1in. | 14ft 1in. |
| Wing area | 260 square ft | 241.5 square ft |
| **Weights** | | |
| Empty | 5,766lb | 4,235lb |
| Loaded | 7,964lb | 5,423lb |
| **Performance** | | |
| Max Speed | 318mph at 19,400ft | 270mph at 15,500ft |
| Range | 830 miles | 715 miles (including auxiliary 330-liter fuel tank) |
| Climb | to 10,000ft in 5 min 40 sec | to 16,400ft in 7 min 42 sec |
| Service Ceiling | 33,700ft | 32,810ft |
| Armament | 6 × 0.50-cal. M2 Browning machine guns | 2 × 7.7mm Type 97 machine guns<br>2 × 20mm Type 99-1 cannon<br>2 × 60kg bombs |

# THE STRATEGIC SITUATION

To understand how Sui-sen were deployed to the remote South Pacific theater, we revert to the Treaty of Versailles in 1919, from which Japan was allocated a vast swathe of Micronesia. Termed the Pacific Mandate, the Japanese isolated the territory, governing it as a military colony and closely regulating contact with the outside world. The IJN divided the area into the five districts of Saipan, Palau, Truk, Ponape, and Jaluit Atoll, all reporting to the Mandate's regional headquarters at Truk. Positioned 800 miles directly north of Rabaul, Truk, in turn, was developed into a huge military base from which Imperial Japan would springboard its supply and logistics into the South Pacific.

Synchronized with its attack against Pearl Harbor, the Japanese struck the Philippines and Malaya on December 7, 1941, delivering decisive blows in the first few days. American, Dutch, and British forces lost considerable ground and assets in a short timeframe. The sinking of two Royal Navy capital ships, in particular, was a shock to the Allies. The battleship HMS *Prince of Wales* and the battlecruiser HMS *Repulse* were both sunk by IJNAF land-attack bombers off the coast of Malaya on December 10, 1941.

The Japanese focus soon turned to planning a Rabaul invasion, first preceded by the capture of Guam and Wake Island. The strategic location of Rabaul, like Truk, boasted an outstanding sheltered and natural harbor, enabling major warships to secure themselves close to shorelines along Simpson Harbor. Rabaul was occupied in January 1942, after which British forces in Singapore capitulated the following month, then the Netherlands East Indies (NEI) in March, with some US forces in the Philippines managing to hold out until May.

The IJN seaplane tender *Kawikawa Maru* sits at anchor off Amoy, China, in July 1939, its deck loaded with E7K2 and E8N2 floatplanes. The vessel was very active in the South Seas campaign three years later, supporting both F1M2 and A6M2-N operations. It was torpedoed and sunk by the submarine USS *Scamp* (SS-277) on May 29, 1943, 250 miles northwest of Kavieng, New Ireland. (Naval History and Heritage Command)

Once ensconced at Rabaul, the IJN took the lead on Japanese expansionism into the South Pacific. It regarded itself as the Imperial "senior service," not only in terms of its elitist training, but also because its personnel were better educated and more cosmopolitan – a concept which held considerable veritas. The IJN looked down on the Imperial Japanese Army (IJA), believing it was manned by lesser individuals and, in more extreme cases, intemperate thugs conditioned by rote and led by ultra-nationalist cliques.

While the IJA highlighted the Soviet Union as Japan's main threat, it exploited China as an opportunity. Meanwhile, the IJN turned to the Pacific, where it forecast that the US Navy would become its principal rival.

When hostilities broke out, the Combined Fleet was an inflexible bureaucracy, guided by around 50 vice-admirals, most of whom had not seen combat and many of whom were approaching retirement. Within this glacial command structure two competing schools of thought sought uncompromising political patronage – the traditional "big gun" battleship exponents set against the "pro-aviation" mostly younger generation, who foresaw a "new world" dominated by powerful aircraft technology.

The initial and primary reason for the Japanese occupation of Rabaul in January 1942 was to prevent its use as an Allied base from which air power could strike Truk. The IJN in turn resolved to protect Rabaul by founding an exterior defense perimeter by occupying Lae, Salamaua, Port Moresby, Bougainville, and Tulagi in the Solomon Islands. From these locations, it was intended that US air power could be checked.

Not short of ambition, and still imbued with "victory disease" from successes in Asia and the Philippines, senior IJN staff officers looked further afield from Rabaul as far as Fiji and Samoa, terming the plan Operation *FS* for their occupation. If triumphant in securing control of these remote expanses, the IJN would make it difficult for US forces to reinforce Australia. As part of this overall strategic plan, the Japanese military unveiled Operation *MO* – the seizure of Port Moresby (the two capital letters representing Moresby) – in early April 1942. As a side operation, the island of Tulagi, with its colonial town of the same name, would also be seized. As an afterthought, an airfield would be built on nearby Guadalcanal that would assist the war aims of Operation *FS*.

At the start of August 1942, Tulagi and Lunga (later Henderson Field) were in Japanese hands. The seaplane base in the Shortland Islands was located midway between Rabaul and Guadalcanal. In addition to seaplane operations, it also served as a logistics hub for ships running supplies to Guadalcanal. A major forward seaplane base was also established at Rekata Bay. The waterway running through the Solomons (i.e. a line from the Shortlands to Henderson Field) became known as "The Slot."

Via code-breaking, US Navy Intelligence correctly deduced Japanese intentions, and checked the advance from Rabaul on Port Moresby. This culminated in the Battle of the Coral Sea, which unfolded in earnest on May 7–8, 1942. Critically, the battle deprived the Combined Fleet of two powerful carriers, *Shokaku* and *Zuikaku*, a month before a planned advance on Midway in early June. Operation *MI* (for Midway) also targeted the Aleutian Islands. The comprehensive defeat of the IJN at Midway put paid to Japanese plans for expansion in the Central Pacific and the hope for a decisive battle against the remaining American carriers.

Meanwhile, for the Japanese the South Seas theater encompassed the entire geographic expanse from New Guinea through to Bougainville and the Solomon Islands. Rabaul, Lae, Salamaua, and Bougainville outposts had been secured in a series of rolling incursions from January through to the end of March 1942 with little or no Allied opposition. After pushing south to Tulagi in May as part of Operation *MO*, the Japanese planned an even greater expansion through Operation *FS*, with a wider and ambitious strategy to include New Caledonia and the New Hebrides along with Fiji and Samoa. However, following the defeat at Midway, plans were recast that foresaw a more prominent role for IJNAF land-based air support using a newly-constructed airfield at Lunga, on Guadalcanal.

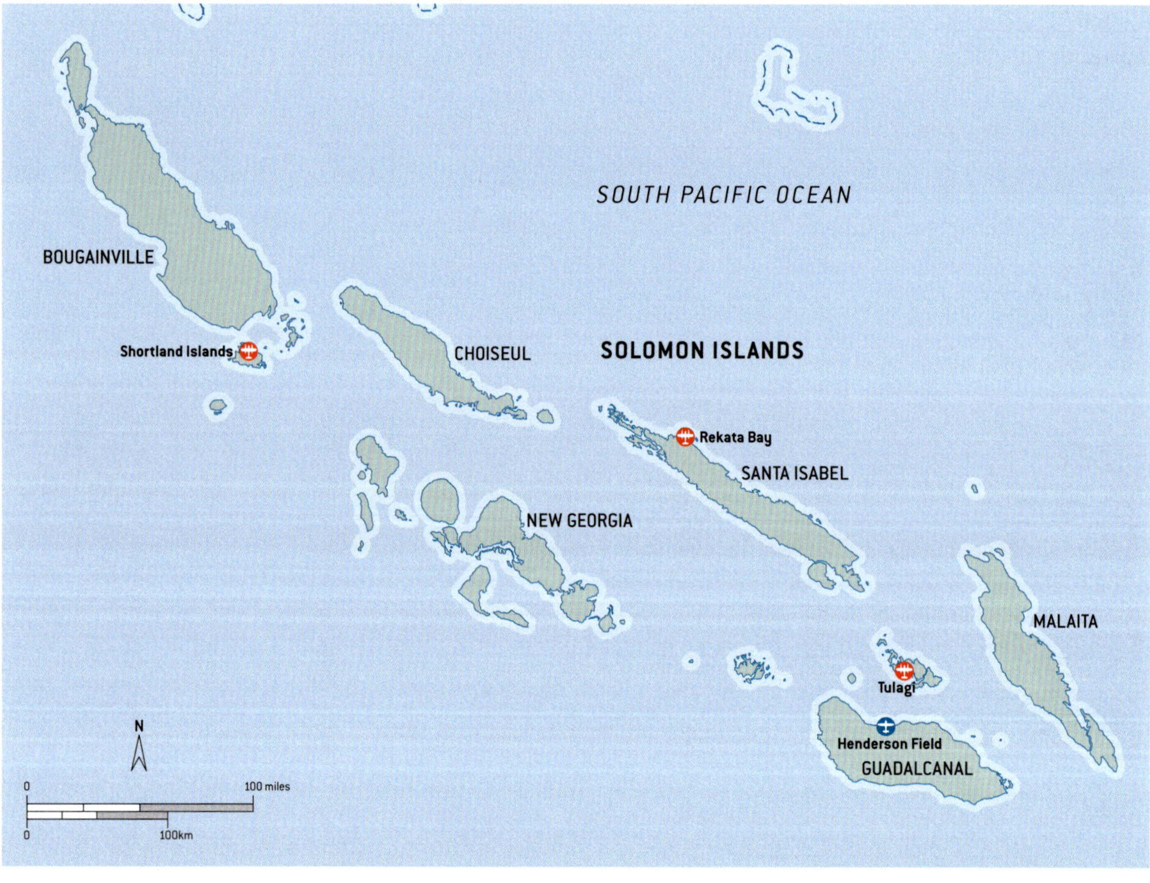

Meanwhile, as part of the Tulagi invasion, floatplanes were stationed briefly in the Shortland Islands and at Rekata Bay. Eventually, substantial barracks and a headquarters complex would be built on Faisi Island (the first island in the Solomons occupied by the Japanese in March 1942) in the Shortlands. The latter were strategically positioned at the midpoint between Rabaul and Tulagi, and support and construction forces commenced building a seaplane base there on April 5 when a Japanese detachment reinforced Faisi Island and nearby Buin. Then on April 28, the merchantmen *Nikkai Maru* and *Seikai Maru* unloaded construction workers and materials on the Shortland Islands.

That same day, five Yokohama Kokutai Kawanishi H6K4 "Mavis" flying boats flew down to the Shortlands from Rabaul, carrying vital communications equipment for the new base. The flying boats subsequently conducted reconnaissance missions from there deep into the Coral Sea and down the Solomon Islands chain. On May 4, fleet oiler *Iro* dropped anchor in the Shortlands to serve as a tanker for deployed Japanese forces in the region, the vessel being accompanied by the destroyer *Uzuki*. Another oiler, *Omurosan Maru*, arrived early the following day, and a third, *Toho Maru*, would also later operate in the area.

Meanwhile, seaplane tender *Kamikawa Maru* sailed further down the Solomons' island chain to Santa Isabel, where it briefly conducted floatplane operations from Rekata Bay on May 2. These were subsequently supported by more floatplanes from *Kiyokawa Maru*. Rekata Bay was around 150 miles from Tulagi, and the floatplanes covered the landing operations there.

Tulagi, opposite Guadalcanal, was the small capital of the British Solomon Islands Protectorate and its main commercial center. The isolated colonial town of small

A pre-war photograph of the British colonial club at Tulagi, later commandeered by the IJN for use as an officers' club following its May 1942 occupation. (Author's Collection)

Rabaul Harbor, seen here under attack from a USAAF B-25 Mitchell in November 1943, was visited almost-daily by H6K4 "Mavis" flying boats in 1942 as they undertook "commuter runs" to the Shortland Islands with spare parts and replacement aircrew. In this photograph, an "Emily" and an E13A1 "Jake" are moored among numerous small ships and barges. (Author's Collection)

wooden buildings was established by the British government on elongated Tulagi Island, which was about two miles long but only several hundred yards wide. Located just offshore much larger Florida Island, and only 20 miles from even larger Guadalcanal, the settlement overlooked a deep harbor. It was from this location that administrative and commercial communications were maintained with the myriad islands that made up the Solomons.

The expatriate civilian population had been evacuated in early February, leaving only a skeleton administrative staff and a handful of plantation owners. However, Tulagi's strategic value was its flying boat base, as no airfields yet existed in the Solomons. The seaplane facility, established by the Royal Australian Air Force (RAAF) in early 1941, lay but a short distance offshore Tulagi on the two tiny islands of Tanambago and Gavutu, which were connected by a causeway. This is where the combat story of the Sui-sen commences, in this desolate yet comparatively comfortable location.

Two Yokohama Kokutai Sui-sen climb out from Halavo in a failed attempt to intercept LB-30 Liberator AL515 of the 19th BG on July 10, 1942 during an armed reconnaissance mission over Tulagi. This was the first photograph taken (by Cpl Charles McBride, using a hand-held K-20 camera) by the Allies of a Sui-sen in combat. (Author's Collection)

Ship-based floatplanes had been ubiquitous throughout the South Seas from the outset of the capture of Rabaul, but not Sui-sen, which were still under development in Japan. When they arrived in-theater, the Sui-sen were the only fighter floatplanes available to the IJNAF, and they were initially deployed in a defensive capacity. The strategic situation quickly changed against Japanese expectations following their deployment, however, wiping out the first Sui-sen detachment and sending replacement units into action against an enemy they had little hope of defeating.

The seizure of Tulagi had been a sideline component of the Battle of the Coral Sea, the fighting of which had stymied Operation *MO* – the capture of Port Moresby. The vessels carrying IJN marines charged with occupying Tulagi arrived offshore during the night of May 2–3, with the mine-layer and flagship *Okinoshima* performing the role of armed transport. Following the occupation, 142 men from Yokohama Kokutai were stationed there, along with several hundred base personnel, all guarded by a modest marine detachment.

The following month, Yokohama Kokutai's Sui-sen forward-deployed to Rabaul, after which they flew on to Tulagi. Here, they commenced air defense patrols, keenly monitored by IJNAF staff officers in Tokyo who read reports of this initial deployment of the Sui-sen with interest. The A6M2-Ns were drawn from the first batch off the Nakajima factory production line, and it was anticipated that critical feedback on the type's combat and operational performance would prove very useful.

Two other bodies with a keen interest in the outcome of the Sui-sen's deployment were Yokosuka Kokutai, the central organization for IJNAF aviation engineering, and the IJNAF Aviation Engineering Department. Whereas the latter was more concerned with modifications to improve performance, Yokosuka Kokutai's advisory role would later determine changes to the training syllabus for Sui-sen pilots.

With support for Operation *FS* much in mind, Vice Adm Shigeyoshi Inoue and Rear Adm Sadayoshi Yamada visited the Lunga airfield construction site on Guadalcanal on June 19, 1942. The fact that the two most senior air commanders in the South Seas journeyed to Guadalcanal at this early, but critical, juncture underlines the strategic importance the IJNAF attached to the developing airfield.

The ability for Solomons-based air power to be projected toward Operation *FS* objectives was demonstrated in early August when two 14th Kokutai "Emily" flying boats used Tulagi as a base from which to conduct two long-range missions over New Caledonia and Fiji. One of these exceeded 16 hours in duration.

Meanwhile, a sizable workforce of foreign labor (principally Formosans), overseen by 11th and 13th Establishment Units, worked day and night at Lunga. Provisioned with sufficient supplies to do the task at hand, work proceeded apace. Japanese construction units throughout the theater depended mostly on paid foreign workers to build airfields, using men such as the Formosans, indentured or slave labor (as was the case on Ballale), or locals, conscripted or otherwise.

At these fields, aircrew slept in damp tents, ate meager food, and generally had a subsistence living. Incapacitated by malaria or dysentery, they worked seven days a week without respite. Dust replaced heavy rain when the soil or coral dried, eroding engines and even causing serious accidents. This meant that progress in the building of any airfield in a remote South Seas location was always going to be slow. As such, seaplane bases looked increasingly attractive as both interim and long-term solutions. The first Sui-sen deployed to the

This photograph of Henderson Field under construction by Formosan workers under Japanese supervision was taken at around midday on July 31, 1942 from 15,000ft by a reconnaissance B-17E. The Lunga River can be seen at the airfield's southern end. (Author's Collection)

Tulagi area were tasked with defending key sites, including Lunga airfield while it was still under construction.

## OPERATION *WATCHTOWER*

Following the resounding US victory at the Battle of Midway in early June, the US Joint Chiefs of Staff initiated the first phase of what would become a major advance toward Rabaul through both New Guinea and the Solomons. The initial plan was crystalized with the discovery of Japanese airfield construction underway at Lunga. Codenamed Operation *Watchtower*, the plan initially included the capture of the Santa Cruz Islands, Tulagi, and Guadalcanal.

US Marines conducted a surprise invasion of both Tulagi and Guadalcanal on August 7, 1942. The timing of the invasion proved judicious for the invaders, as Lunga airfield was scheduled to be declared operational that very day. In fact, an H6K4 "Mavis" had been scheduled to transport senior 11th Air Fleet officers from Rabaul to Tulagi the previous day to inspect the runway. However, the visit had been delayed due to a serviceability issue, doubtless saving the lives of those manifested on the flight. A crude 200ft x 2,600ft runway carved out of a plantation at Lunga was capable of handling fighters, although the A6M2-equipped 6th Kokutai, slated to be the first one stationed there, was still training in Japan at the time.

August 7, 1942 also saw the first Wildcat/Sui-sen engagement – a one-sided affair that wiped out the South Seas A6M2-N unit without any aerial air combat actually taking place. This occurred when 11 F4F-4s from VF-71, embarked in *Wasp*, were led by the unit CO, Lt Cdr Courtney Shands, over the Tulagi area in a low-level sweep as part of the Guadalcanal invasion. The US Navy pilots executed their attack 15 minutes before sunrise, when the Yokohama Kokutai Sui-sen were fueled, armed, and ready for their first morning patrols. Moored along the beach at Halavo, on Florida Island, the floatplane fighters were destroyed with incendiary rounds – as were a pair on the nearby Gavutu Island slipway. The surprise attack effectively wiped out the entire Yokohama Kokutai, which also lost seven H6K4s.

The invasion of Guadalcanal triggered a knee-jerk response from the Japanese, forcing them to fight in both New Guinea and the Solomons. More importantly, it also caused them to postpone plans for further territorial expansion in the South Pacific. Meanwhile, all operational decisions involving air power stemmed from the local IJNAF HQ in Rabaul, which assessed in reaction to the American invasion of August 7 that the

An F4F-4 Wildcat, with wings folded, destined for Guadalcanal is transferred from the aircraft transport USS *Kitty Hawk* (AKV-1) to the escort carrier USS *Long Island* (AVG-1) at Port Vila, in the New Hebrides, in August 1942. The latter vessel delivered the first aircraft (19 Wildcats and 12 Dauntlesses) to reach Henderson Field. (Author's Collection)

reconquest of Tulagi and Guadalcanal could quickly be accomplished. 11th Air Fleet HQ thus saw no compelling urgency to build staging airfields in the central Solomons, especially when the New Guinea area was also commanding extra resources at short notice with military distractions at Buna and Milne Bay.

Personnel from a US Naval Construction Battalion, better known as Seabees, set about expanding Henderson Field in early September 1942. The extended northern end of the airfield cut through a copra plantation owned by British manufacturing company Lever Brothers. (Author's Collection)

When it became apparent that the struggle for Henderson Field (formerly Lunga airfield) would become more protracted than it wished, 11th Air Fleet looked at alternatives for air support. IJNAF strategic planners remained focused on the potential of the Shortlands to become a major seaplane base, for it was protected from prevailing winds and boasted unobstructed deep channels. A series of adjoining islands also offered potential for a diverse suite of military facilities. The area's anchorages later became a model for seaplane operations, catering for all types ranging from single-seat Sui-sen to the large and state-of-the-art four-engined H8K2 "Emily" flying boat.

Despite the critical loss of four carriers at Midway, the IJN still exercised local naval superiority throughout the South Pacific for the rest of 1942. While the American intrusion at Guadalcanal was triumphant, their initial advantage left their forces exposed to counterattack. In the months following the invasion, both sides committed resources to the area. Soon the alien name "Guadalcanal" became the front page headline in US newspapers – it was equally famous in the Japanese press as "Guadukanaru."

With 11th Air Fleet at Rabaul finding itself heavily engaged on two geographical fronts from August onwards, the Guadalcanal air campaign started proving more punitive to the IJNAF. Forced to conduct attacks at a punishing range of 600 miles, land-based units were severely impeded in their flexibility and operational deployment. It also predicated and limited the types of bomb loads that could be delivered, and constrained time for aerial combat.

Floatplanes were not so restricted operationally because they did not need runways. The availability of vast mooring areas in the Shortlands and at Rekata Bay duly led to the rapid creation of the R-Area Force, as later detailed. Floatplane fighters assigned to it initially opposed B-17s targeting IJNAF airfields and IJN ports and facilities in the region, although the R-Area Force's A6M2-Ns and other single-engined floatplanes soon began to be used more innovatively for raids on Henderson Field. In reality, however, such cursory attacks were incapable of inflicting noteworthy damage. This was due primarily to the floatplanes' limited bomb payload, but also because there were so few examples available in-theater.

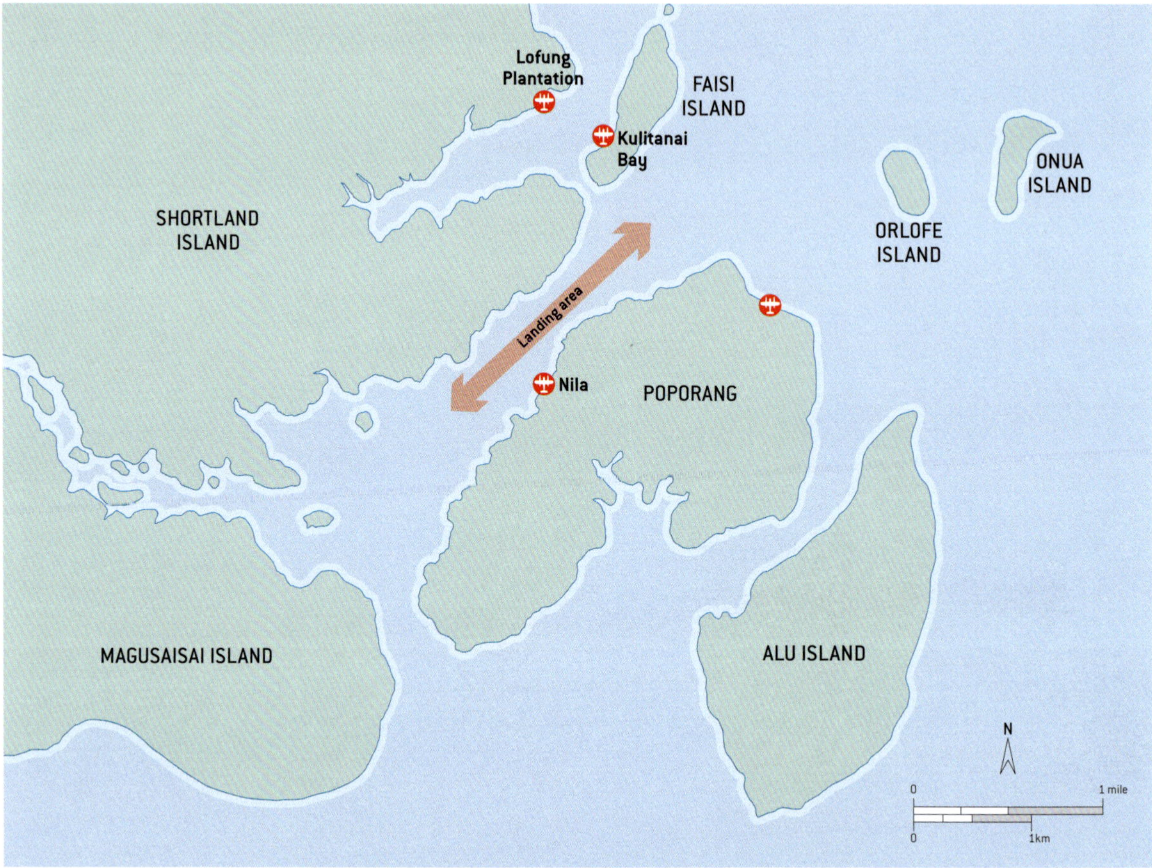


Then, at the end of September, B-17Es started using Henderson Field, which expanded their range to Tonolei Harbor in the Shortlands, and also the latter's seaplane moorings. At this time, overall aircraft losses in August–September 1942 in the Guadalcanal campaign were closely matched – 192 Allied aircraft versus 203 Japanese aircraft lost.

This difficult two-month period transformed the thinking of 11th Air Fleet at Rabaul. 4th Kokutai, which had fought in the theater from the start, had lost 52 Mitsubishi G4M1 "Betty" bombers (almost double its normal complement) in that short period of time. The remnants of the depleted unit were withdrawn in September, as were the surviving "Mavis" flying boats of Yokohama Kokutai, its fighter wing decimated at Tulagi as described. The elite Tainan Kokutai had lost most of its pilot cadre, and its remaining Zero-sen inventory was parceled out to other units when the surviving aviators were returned to Japan to create a replacement Kokutai.

IJNAF aircrew losses in the same period constituted a more serious matter than the destruction of airframes – a substantive 517, averaging ten lost per day, contrasted against Allied losses of 92. The Japanese loss rate was unsustainable, the lesser Allied losses rationalized by the fact that crews normally bailed out over friendly territory. Due to the assistance and influence of Australian Coastwatchers, nearly every Solomon Islander was on standby to help any downed Allied pilot. The exception were the villages around southern Bougainville, including the Shortlands, where a downed

Coastwatcher Maj Martin Clemens (a District Officer in the British Solomon Islands Protectorate Defence Force) briefs one of his scouts at Henderson Field in late August 1942. After the Japanese occupied Tulagi in early May 1942, they unsuccessfully initiated searches for Clemens, who subsequently provided invaluable intelligence to US forces throughout the Guadalcanal campaign. (Author's Collection)

Sui-sen pilot could expect friendly treatment. In nearly all other parts of the Solomons, Japanese pilots could at best be expected to be taken prisoner, although often they were simply killed.

The end of September 1942 saw the Guadalcanal campaign in the balance, with the Japanese planning another major land offensive for October. Like so many junctures in this critical theater of war, fate was poised to fall either way. In mid-September the IJN had established a substantial Daihatsu barge and floatplane base at Wickham anchorage, inserted into the southern tip of Vangunu – a large island positioned on the southern tip of New Georgia in the Solomon Islands. A modest seaplane base on Gizo Island, some 30 miles northeast of Munda, had also been established. However, both locations were heavily bombed by the Cactus Air Force (the name by which Allied air power on Guadalcanal was known from August 1942) throughout October, and as a result neither were ever used by Sui-sen as a base.

## R-AREA FORCE

The R in "R-Area Force" represents Rabaul, the overall term deriving from the Japanese phrase "R-Homen Koku Butai." This floatplane collective was created on August 28, 1942 as a direct response to the American landings at Tulagi and Guadalcanal three weeks earlier. Its commander was Rear Adm Takatsugu Jojima, who was already leading 11th Seaplane Tender Division – an incumbency he had held since June 20, 1942. Jojima was an experienced naval aviator, and had previously served as

**OPPOSITE PAGE**
The Shortland Islands seaplane base where Rear Adm Takatsugu Jojima, commander 11th Seaplane Tender Division, based his forward-deployed floatplanes known as the R-Area Force. Only five nautical miles south of the IJNAF airfield on the island of Ballale, these four anchorages were ideal for supporting all manner of seaplane operations ranging in size from single-engined floatplanes up to four-engined flying boats. Protected from prevailing winds, and with unobstructed deep channels, the three proximate islands housed a diversified complex. Floatplanes were anchored off Shortland Island itself, while just 100m across the channel, a substantial accommodation complex was built on Faisi. By early 1943, workshop and support facilities had been constructed at Bambagiai Plantation across the narrow southern channel between Faisi and Shortland Island, and a regular launch service plied between other islands in the vicinity, including Ballale. AA guns were scattered throughout the complex and on the surrounding hills.

Henderson Field in August–September 1942. The building in the background, built by the IJN, was dubbed "The Pagoda." It served as headquarters for the 1st Marine Air Wing (which controlled all aviation on Guadalcanal) until razed to the ground in mid-October to prevent the wooden structure from being of further use to IJA gunners as a range marker when sighting artillery prior to shelling Henderson Field. (NARA)

captain of the aircraft carriers *Shoho* and *Hiryu*. He led R-Area Force until it was disestablished on April 15, 1943.

The force was an administrative concept, its operational component remaining 11th Seaplane Tender Division, albeit expanded and modified. Operationally, it was divided into two wings. The Force, which brought together aircraft (including Sui-sen) from tenders and shore-based units, was based on the strategic concept that the versatility of floatplanes would compensate for the lack of airfields in-theater.

R-Area Force grew as reinforcement detachments of engineers and equipment set up at shore bases at Rabaul and Kavieng, and in the Solomons – mainly on Poporang and Faisi Islands, in the Shortland Islands, where nearby Tonolei Harbor was the primary staging area for resupply convoys heading to Guadalcanal. A forward floatplane base was also established at Rekata Bay. This location provided strategic proximity to Japanese troops fighting on Guadalcanal unavailable to land-based aircraft. R-Area Force floatplanes initially focused on performing combat air patrol (CAPs) and covering IJN supply convoys navigating the waters of "The Slot" (New Georgia Sound) on supply runs to Guadalcanal.

The seaplane base at Rekata Bay was a key asset for R-Area Force in late 1942, the site offering both dispersed beach access and inland cantonment for seaplane operations. The area also provided effective camouflage under which to secure supplies, parts, and airframes. On September 5, the seaplane tender *Akitsushima* significantly provisioned the base, providing it with a refueling capability. Now heavily defended by anti-aircraft (AA) guns, the upgraded facilities gave R-Area Force floatplanes the ability to strike Henderson Field.

However, Rekata Bay also fell within reciprocal range of the Cactus Air Force. This persuaded the IJNAF to stage its floatplanes through the base overnight, departing in the early hours to avoid daylight attacks – R-Area Force's

*modus operandi* was to evacuate valuable aircraft to the relative safety of the Shortlands.

Floatplane missions from Rekata against Henderson Field soon proved a nuisance to the Allies. However, no bombs could damage Rekata Bay's ever-present beach, which served as an unsinkable mooring platform for R-Area Force. When the Japanese evacuated Guadalcanal in February 1943, Rabaul determined that the Rekata garrison should be bolstered to defend it. Accordingly, the 7th Special Naval Landing Force was sent there, later complemented by an IJA battalion. By the end of July 1943 some 3,400 personnel were stationed at Rekata Bay, underlining just how important this facility was to the IJNAF.

During its brief period of existence, R-Area Force was frequently restructured due to seaplane tender reassignments, changing floatplane inventories, and mission changes. CAPs for resupply convoys emanated from both the Shortlands and

The seaplane tender *Chitose*, with a pair of E8N2s attached to its stern, was heavily involved in operations (particularly in the South Seas) from December 1941 through to January 1943, when work commenced on its conversion into a light aircraft carrier. No Sui-sen were ever embarked onboard the vessel, however, the *Chitose* buntai operating F1M2s and E13A1s. (Public Domain)

Sui-sen YII-104 and YII-105 aboard *Kamikawa Maru* during its return delivery voyage to the Shortland Islands in September 1942. Note the wooden aileron restraints for the voyage and the protective rubber matting cover on YII-104's main float – this machine is having its engine run. The unit markings (fuselage stripes and red tail codes) were applied to the aircraft in Japan prior to their departure for the South Seas. (Tony Holmes Collection)

Rekata Bay, exacting a heavy toll on the R-Area Force. The seaplane tenders *Chitose* and *Nisshin* played the role of high-speed transports alongside the destroyers throughout October, carrying heavy equipment which the smaller warships could not. At times, the protection of these tenders became a critical mission for attentive floatplanes.

By September 12, R-Area Force's First Air Wing comprised the *Chitose* buntai of 16 F1M2 "Petes" and seven E13A1 "Jakes" commanded by Lt Takeshi Horibata, complemented by the *Kamikawa Maru* buntai comprising two "Petes" and 11 Sui-sen under Lt Jiro Ono. The Second Air Wing was made up of six "Petes" and two "Jakes" from *Sanyo Maru* under Lt Tadashi Yoneda, with *Sanuki Maru* contributing six "Petes" led by Lt(jg) Kaneshige Watanabe.

Throughout September–October, R-Area Force losses were particularly heavy through aerial combat while covering delivery convoys. By October 4, its inventory had been reduced to 12 F1M2 "Petes," five Sui-sen, and nine E13A1 "Jakes" from the *Chitose* and *Sanyo Maru* air detachments. On October 12, 14th Kokutai's fighter wing joined the R-Area Force at Poporang Island following the delivery of nine Sui-sen to Rabaul by *Kiyokawa Maru*. More floatplanes were added around this time, including two additional "Petes," two more "Jakes," and nine antiquated Kawanishi E7K "Alf" and "Dave" biplane floatplanes used for regional liaison.

The ongoing depletion of the inventory had reached near-crisis levels by mid-November when no floatplane replacements were forthcoming. This was because the seaplane tenders *Kamikawa Maru* and *Sanyo Maru* had been reallocated to transporting equipment for major offensives on Guadalcanal. Then, on November 13, *Sanuki Maru* delivered eight more "Petes" from Yokosuka.

While most IJNAF land-based units were restructured on November 1, 1942, several R-Area Force units were not restructured until December 1. During the planned withdrawal from Guadalcanal in Operation *Ke* throughout January and into early February 1943, the R-Area Force performed the dual roles of air cover and reconnaissance.

The R-Area Force denoted its bases via three-letter codes beginning with the letter "R" – e.g. RWH was Shortland Harbor, RWI was nearby Tonolei Harbor, and RWO was Shortland Bay. By early 1943, an overhaul workshop had been built on nearby Bambagiai Island. IJN patrol boats plied the waters regularly between the islands, and once a day up to the airfield base on Ballale Island, shuttling supplies and technicians. AA batteries were scattered in the hills behind and throughout the complex. Engineering facilities were established on Faisi Island, where around 300 aircrew and support personnel were also based. "Mavis" seaplanes ran regular return shuttles to Rabaul, these flights lasting about three hours. The seaplanes were loaded and offloaded inside Malaguna Bay, returning to the Shortlands with provisions, parts, medicines, replacement crews, and sometimes VIPs.

As some of R-Area Force's primary opponents, the Wildcat-equipped units on Guadalcanal gradually moved from their primary duty of protecting Henderson Field from attacks by G4M1 "Betty" bombers to venturing further afield to escort Grumman TBF Avengers and Douglas SBD Dauntlesses attacking the regular destroyer supply runs dubbed the "Tokyo Express."

R-Area Force Sui-sen are readied for their next patrol whilst moored in the shallows of Rekata Bay in late 1942, with Papatura Island seen in the distance. The wartime censor has removed all tail codes from these aircraft. Such aircraft, devoid of any camouflage and sat exposed and in the open, were highly vulnerable to strafing attacks by American fighters. (Author's Collection)

By late 1942, the Wildcats were also turning their attention to raids on Rekata Bay, only 160 miles from Henderson Field. This turned into a cat-and-mouse game, with regular dawn raids against the base trying to catch floatplanes at their moorings. To foil these attacks, R-Area Force would often use Rekata Bay during the day and then return its fighters to the safety of the Shortlands overnight to avoid the dawn strikes. The 400-mile, three-hour roundtrip to the Shortlands and then back to Rekata Bay meant the use of more precious fuel, increased pilot fatigue, and the chance of being attacked en route by Wildcats. When Rekata Bay was eventually captured in late 1943, the new occupiers found only one derelict Sui-sen airframe.

Guadalcanal-based Wildcats had the advantage of an early warning system in the form of a comprehensive Coastwatcher network. In the lead-up to hostilities, Cdr Eric Feldt of the Royal Australian Navy had established an observer network of civilians equipped with radios. The Coastwatchers comprised former plantation owners and colonial officers, all of whom had intimate knowledge of both the geography and the local peoples.

Furthermore, US Marine Corps radar systems near Henderson Field were able to detect IJNAF formations about 140 miles away, granting scrambling Wildcat pilots the critical time needed to climb to higher altitude before carrying out diving attacks. This radar was not as effective against smaller formations, however, particularly if they approached at low altitudes. Floatplane pilots knew this, and accordingly approached Henderson Field at low altitude for surprise attacks.

# THE COMBATANTS

## US NAVY AND US MARINE CORPS TRAINING

In early 1942, the US Navy and US Marine Corps halved the length of their Primary flying course down to about six months. Like many similar services worldwide, fresh students received physical training, were taught basic navy etiquette, and undertook ten to 15 hours of flying instruction which led to their first solo.

US Navy and US Marine Corps would-be fighter pilots began their Primary flight training on biplane primary trainers in the form of the Naval Aircraft Factory N3N or the Boeing-Stearman N2S, with examples of both types being seen here. The primary trainers were christened the "Yellow Peril" due to their bright color scheme, with these particular aircraft being based at NAS Corpus Christi, Texas, in 1942–43. (Public Domain)

Importantly, the lead-up to World War II had witnessed a pivotal transferal of training away from floatplanes, which had so epitomized US Navy thinking during the early interwar years, to land-based, carrier-capable aircraft. During this era, the staid V-5 Naval Reserve program took 18 months to complete. Following graduation, alumni were then required to complete three years of active duty with the lowly rank of Aviation Cadet, after which they were eligible for promotion to the coveted rank of lieutenant in the US Navy Reserve. In June 1939, US Congress radically altered the program so that cadets received commissions as ensigns or junior grade lieutenants after only a year of training, before proceeding to Naval Air Station (NAS) Pensacola, Florida, for further flight training.

Once at Pensacola, cadets completed a further 80 hours of instruction on Boeing-Stearman N2S or Naval Aircraft Factory N3N biplanes, with both types being christened the "Yellow Peril" due to their bright color scheme – coincidentally, a scheme they shared with their IJNAF counterparts. The follow-on Intermediate phase, undertaken in the Curtiss SNC or Vultee SNV Valiant, intended to transform the cadet into a military pilot by instilling combat tactics, with focused instrument training undertaken in the Link Trainer. Latter stages of instruction included formation and night flying, during which pilots slated for carrier operations trained on the North American SNJ Texan, with which they made numerous simulated carrier landings on concrete runways marked accordingly. Navigation and intermediate combat tactics, including gunnery, completed the course.

After completing their Primary and Basic intermediate training phases, US Navy aviation cadets selected for carrier-based types moved on to fly the Curtiss SNC (foreground and middle) and the North American SNJ (background) in Advanced intermediate training. (NARA)

Yet by the early 1940s, most prospective US Navy and US Marine Corps pilots were still entering flight training through the pre-war V-5 Naval Reserve program. Secretary of Navy Frank Knox anticipated, and planned for, an extended war, during which an adequate supply of replacement pilots for frontline duty could be guaranteed. Accordingly, and following the outbreak of hostilities, Knox expanded the US Navy flight training program to produce 20,000 Naval Aviators annually. This concept was force-multiplied when the first batches of returning combat pilots were begrudgingly assigned as instructors to pass on hard-won experience.

At the beginning of 1941, the target output for pilot graduates was increased to 2,500 per month. Shortly thereafter, the US Navy also decided to establish its own operational training units to provide specialist advanced tuition on specific aircraft types. Prior to this, students had been taught to fly a variety of different carrier aircraft types. Aside from carrier operations, around 300 hours of tuition also covered aerial gunnery and combat tactics, dive-bombing and torpedo delivery. Advanced Carrier Training groups were authorized from July 1941 to provide additional training in operating the latest combat types, and adapting advanced fighter tactics to suit different aircraft.

To accelerate graduate output, the requirement to have pilots capable of flying all three categories of carrier aircraft was waived. Instead, students were streamed into one of the three categories of US Navy aircraft types – fighters, dive-bombers, or torpedo-bombers.

Once fighter graduates reached advanced training, both the US Navy and US Marine Corps focused heavily on the critical importance of aerial gunnery, including deflection shooting. The syllabus emphasized two key elements to aerial gunnery – when to fire and where to aim. Having estimated the proper lead, pilots were taught to open fire at a distance of 1,000ft from the target, then continue firing as they closed to an optimal range of between 200–300ft. Following extensive mathematical and physics theory in the classroom and

Aviation cadets began practicing aerial gunnery in Advanced intermediate training in order to learn standard gunnery approaches. Flying SNJs armed with a 0.30-cal. machine gun, cadets fired color-coded rounds at the target sleeve – they are shown here counting up their hits. (NARA)

The Gunairstructor was a synthetic training device (a precursor of the flight simulator) developed to train pilots in aerial gunnery. It replicated the cockpit of a fighter, with the sounds of the engine and the firing of the guns for greater verisimilitude. In the Gunairstructor, a pilot could practice gunnery approaches and deflection shooting against a target projected onto a screen in front of the cockpit. (NARA)

sessions in the Gunairstructor sythentic training device, students undertook relentless practice in the air. These sessions stressed teamwork and how to gain tactical advantage before commencing combat. The end result, it was hoped, was to maximize the destruction of enemy aircraft.

After earning his Wings of Gold, and having accumulated about 600 hours of flight time (including around 200 hours on frontline aircraft types), a newly-minted US Navy fighter pilot was assigned to a carrier unit, whereas his US Marine Corps counterpart was posted to a Marine Corps Air Station (MCAS) in Florida for more operational training. Here, pilots trained on worn F4F-3 Wildcats, receiving yet further instruction in gunnery, night flying, carrier landings, combat tactics, and cross-country navigation. Gunnery practice included live ammunition passes at tow-target sleeves using color-coded rounds.

## MORALE

The average age of a Wildcat pilot serving in the Solomons was 22. In combat zones, both the US Navy and US Marine Corps skilfully boosted morale by recognizing good service via the awarding of air medals to those deemed worthy. It is not surprising that under such circumstances healthy competition arose between pilots to earn the most "kills." Although this situation contributed toward exaggerated scores, its main purpose of maintaining functioning pilots and raising their morale was achieved.

For those American pilots sent to the Solomons, their "quality of life" in-theater depended on their service. It was commonly accepted that the best-fed and accommodated units were those of the US Navy, followed by their US Marine Corps counterparts, with the USAAF a poor third. The Japanese did their best, with considerable effectiveness, to interrupt sleep on Guadalcanal through the mounting of regular night raids and incursions. At Guadalcanal, "Washing Machine Charlie" or "Louie the Louse" in the form of solo floatplanes or bombers late at night or in early morning darkness were never welcome visitors.

The Wildcat's legendary strength and protection for fuel and pilot, and its commensurate ability to withstand combat damage, proved a real fillip to the morale of Guadalcanal's US Navy/US Marine Corps fighter cadre. Their counterparts in the Sui-sen had no armor protection for the pilot or self-sealing fuel tanks, which meant the floatplane fighter could not withstand sustained combat damage. The Sui-sen pilot, therefore, had a much greater chance of perishing or being seriously wounded in aerial combat, whereas an F4F-4 pilot often survived the shooting up of his aircraft. The three top US Marine Corps Wildcat aces at Guadalcanal, Capts Marion Carl and Joe Foss and Maj John Smith, were all shot down at some stage but returned to fight again.

## F4F-4 WILDCAT TACTICS

Right through from the US Guadalcanal/Tulagi invasion of August 7, 1942 until mid-February 1943, US Marine Corps and US Navy Wildcats and IJNAF Sui-sen fought each other in the Solomons. Prior to the Pacific War, US Navy/US Marine Corps fighter tactical doctrine employed the three-aircraft vic as the basic combat formation. In response to Royal Air Force (RAF) combat reports produced from fighting the Luftwaffe, the US Navy experimented with two-aircraft formations from mid-1940, assigning the leader as attacker, with a wingman to protect him.

VF-2 and VF-5 were tasked with trialing the new technique, but it took another year before the US Navy adopted the concept. This resulted in the standard US Navy squadron of 18 fighters being divided into three divisions of six machines, with each division then being broken down into three two-aircraft flights. Increased flightdeck space on carriers became available when the folding-wing F4F-4 was introduced into service in early 1942. This enabled Wildcat squadrons to increase their complement to 27, but retain six-fighter divisions.

In 1941, the gunnery officer (and future CO) of VF-3, Lt John Thach, digested an intelligence assessment which suggested that, compared with the Wildcat, the Zero-sen had superiority in speed, rate-of-climb, and rate-of-turn. Under such circumstances, Thach assessed that the Wildcat's only advantages were its firepower and the gunnery prowess of its pilot – qualities which could be exploited if suitable tactics were adapted. He laid out a suite of options for Wildcat formations to achieve this, implementing and then trialing his ideas in the training environment.

Thach designed a concept which gave the Wildcat one brief but pivotal opportunity to land a decisive volley into an enemy. This was achieved by having two sections positioned at a distance equal to the diameter of their tightest turning circle, enabling either fighter to defensively turn into each other when attacked. Thach's scissoring tactic had the added advantage that it needed no radio communication between pilots once the maneuver had been reinforced at the practical level.

Despite the Grumman fighter's success in 1942, Thach remained critical of the overall performance of the F4F-4. His after-action report from Midway concludes that any successes gained by the Wildcat in the battle were mostly attributable to the pilot's superior marksmanship and team work. Indeed, gunnery and teamwork continued to be common themes emphasized time and again to the Guadalcanal Wildcat pilots, with the most common tactic being the high-altitude ambush. This was only achievable in cases where sufficient warning or surprise were received.

A division of six US Marine Corps F4F-4 Wildcats heads off on a mission from Guadalcanal in January 1943. From early 1942, the standard US Navy/US Marine Corps squadron of 18 fighters (increased to 27 with the advent of the folding-wing F4F-4) was usually divided into three divisions of six aircraft, with each division then being broken down into three two-aircraft flights. (Author's Collection)

However, many encounters with Sui-sen were unexpected, and under these circumstances the Wildcat faced a curious challenge. Although the floatplane fighter was slower than the Zero-sen, it had nearly as much maneuverability. This meant that although a

# F4F-4 WILDCAT COCKPIT

1. Clock
2. Cylinder head temperature gauge
3. Rudder pedal adjustment lever
4. Propeller control
5. Ignition switch
6. Propeller selector switch
7. Emergency electrical fuel pump switch
8. Check-off switch
9. Carburetor air control
10. Altimeter
11. Directional gyro
12. Padded electrical Mk 8 gunsight
13. Airspeed indicator
14. Turn-and-bank indicator
15. Rate-of-climb indicator
16. Gyro horizon
17. Manifold pressure gauge
18. Tachometer
19. Outside air temperature
20. Fuel quantity gauge
21. Primer pump
22. Cowl flaps hand crank
23. Engine temperature gauge
24. Compass
25. Oil dilution switch
26. Radio signal light
27. Electric wiring diagram
28. Fuel tank selector valve
29. Rudder tab control
30. Aileron tab control
31. Throttle control
32. Recognition lights switch
33. Mixture control
34. Elevator tab control
35. Arresting hook control
36. Starter switch
37. Tailwheel castor lock
38. Friction adjusting knob
39. Gunsight light rheostat
40. Electrical distribution panel and switch box
41. Fuse panel spare fuses and bulbs under door
42. Gun charging handle
43. Landing gear hand crank
44. Electric circuit breaker reset buttons
45. Control column
46. Pilot's seat
47. Pilot's seat belts
48. Cockpit lighting
49. Rudder pedals
50. Fire extinguisher handle

Wildcat could easily outrun a Sui-sen, the teamwork and tactics used by F4F-4 pilots were harder to employ when an A6M2-N was darting all over the sky – IJNAF floatplane fighter pilots relied heavily on evasive tactics. Frequently, a Wildcat pilot withdrew from combat convinced he had downed a Sui-sen when, in fact, his opponent had instead feinted a steep dive toward the water below and then cruised back to base at low-level.

*Saratoga*, its flightdeck crowded with Wildcats and Dauntlesses, sails into Pearl Harbor on June 6, 1942, having departed San Diego, California, five days earlier. Aside from the 37 aircraft on the flightdeck, a further 61 were jammed into the hangar bay. The *Saratoga* Air Group was heavily involved in the early attacks on Guadalcanal and nearby islands on August 7, and its aircraft (including those of VF-5) eventually went ashore to Henderson Field after the carrier was damaged by a torpedo at month-end. (Public Domain)

On August 20, 1942, the first US Marine Corps fighter squadron arrived at Henderson Field in the form of VMF-223, commanded by Capt John Smith, with 19 F4F-4s. VMF-224 soon followed under Maj Robert Galer, then on September 11, following damage to the carrier USS *Saratoga* (CV-3) on August 31, VF-5 CO Lt Cdr Leroy Simpler led 24 F4F-4s from Espiritu Santo to Henderson Field for a tour of land-based operations.

At this stage in the Pacific War, the enshrined doctrine for these early squadrons was to avoid dogfighting nimble Japanese fighters. However, as Guadalcanal's Wildcat pilots grew in their proficiency, they adopted more aggressive tactics. They now stuck together in pairs as much as possible, having initially climbed to intercept enemy aircraft as a group. Formations were tightly held at higher altitudes to avoid individuals becoming separated. Following a pass made against an enemy aircraft, if there was opportunity to re-climb, then pilots would do so. If a Wildcat suffered "blower" (supercharger) failure or had engine problems during the climb, the pilot would head to the eastern end of Guadalcanal, where he would wait out any air raids in progress before returning to Henderson Field.

While serving as Executive Officer of VMF-121, Capt Joseph Foss accumulated an impressive score against both Zero-sen and Sui-sen. He later attributed this success to his study of Lt Cdr Jimmy Flatley's manual on fighter tactics during the sea voyage from California to the Solomons in September–October 1942. In his autobiography, Foss describes that he was usually successful if he was able to get close to his opponent before opening fire. If he was denied the opportunity of surprise, he would "play chicken" with his opponent instead, flying at him head on and waiting until the enemy pulled up to avoid collision. With the target aircraft exposed, Foss would fire into the wing root.

He enjoyed success against the A6M2-N on November 7, 1942, claiming a "Float Zero" destroyed along with two other "Float biplanes." He subsequently gave his impressions of fighting such aircraft in April 1943 after completing his tour at Henderson Field:

An F4F-4 from VMF-121 undergoes maintenance in the open at Henderson Field in late 1942. The rugged Wildcat stood up well to the rigors of combat in the Solomons, with its Pratt & Whitney R-1830-86/90 engine proving particularly robust. (Author's Collection)

> . . . they buzz around – they'll turn on a dime. I saw five P-39s chasing one, one day. They had just started to shoot when he decided that was enough of that, so he turned around and came head-on back out. The P-39s scattered and went in all directions. Then they made another run, and when he'd seen them all bearing down on him and start shooting, he'd made a quick turn and jumped right back through them, nearly causing them to have a collision with each other. They were all so crazy to get him that they chased him for 15 minutes before they finally got him.
>
> Another morning, my flight ran into two of them, and all seven of the boys turned off after one. I had the other one to myself. I didn't want to fool around with him, so I gave him a burst and he started smoking. I thought I had him. I then raced over to get this other one that they were chasing. I started over and looked back. The one that I thought I'd got was taking off again up the channel.

After a while, Foss's persistent accomplishments, and that of his fellow pilots, started to influence the mindset on Guadalcanal. This revised thinking on aggressive maneuvering with IJNAF fighters translated through into Wildcat tactics for the rest of the war. When Lt Col Joe Bauer became the fighter leader of the Cactus Air Force on October 17, he told his pilots henceforth that they were to challenge enemy fighters head-on, then use the F4F-4's superior firepower to knock them down. Nonetheless, in the end for the Wildcat pilots of Guadalcanal, it always came back to teamwork and good gunnery.

This quality is underlined by the combat reports of VF-5, gifting us with a detailed synopsis of the experiences and appraisals of 11 Wildcat pilots who encountered Sui-sen for the first time on September 14, 1942. Their accounts proffer an excellent barometer of comparative combat performance between the Zero-sen and its close cousin, the Sui-sen. The VF-5 pilots had already acquired a month's experience fighting the A6M2 in the Solomons, giving more weight to their impressions of engaging Sui-sen.

VF-5 CO Lt Cdr Leroy Simpler, having led a one-sided combat against a formation of outnumbered Sui-sen, concluded that the floatplane fighter was slightly inferior to the F4F-4 in performance. Lt Walter Clarke assessed the Sui-sen as slower than the F4F-4, although more maneuverable. Lt(jg) Elisha Stover also thought the F4F-4 was generally superior, noting that the Sui-sen could nonetheless outclimb it. Conversely, Lt(jg) Howard Grimmell's stated that he thought the Sui-sen was faster than his Wildcat, and also more maneuverable. He underlined that this was true even though the Sui-sen were "hopelessly overwhelmed by us."

Ens John Wesolowski dove on the first of four "float Zeros" he encountered, swinging in behind one of them. He then discovered to his alarm that the Sui-sen was sufficiently maneuverable to turn straight back at him! During a second head-on pass, Wesolowski was amazed to see his attacker roll over onto his back and commence a dive. Ens George Morgan's assessment was that the Sui-sen were "good, fast, but could not perform as well as the Zero."

In this staged press photograph, VMF-121 ace Capt Joe Foss poses with two armorers at Henderson Field in 1942. Each of the magazines for the F4F-4's six M2 machine guns could hold 240 rounds. (Public Domain)

VF-5 pilots also stated that their opponents in the Zero-sen and Sui-sen often overshot during stern attacks, forcing them to recover ahead of the Wildcat – US Marine Corps pilots flying from Henderson Field noted this trait too. Both types were then briefly vulnerable to a burst from the Wildcat's six 0.50-cal. machine guns before the Sui-sen pilot had time to initiate a sharp turn. On the other hand, the A6M2-N had almost no chance to counteract Wildcat "hit and run" tactics. Finally, but critically, when a Sui-sen did manage to catch a Wildcat, pilots were then thwarted by the Grumman fighter's ability to absorb punishing fire.

While many fighter pilots decried the reduction in ammunition associated with the increase from four 0.50-cal. machine guns in the F4F-3 to six such weapons in the F4F-4, a close-range burst from either Wildcat variant proved devastating for the Sui-sen's unprotected fuel tanks. While the Sui-sen's 20mm projectile was heavier and more destructive than a 0.50-cal. bullet, the weight of ammunition from a two-second burst by the Sui-sen's twin Type 99-1 cannon was comparatively less than a two-second burst from the six more rapidly firing M2 machine guns installed in the F4F-4.

This F4F-4 was one of seven sortied by VMF-121 (and four by VMO-251) before dawn on November 1, 1942 and sent to attack Rekata Bay floatplane base – a favorite target of the Cactus Air Force, for it was easily identifiable and within Wildcat range of Guadalcanal. All of the F4Fs involved received varying degrees of damage from the light-caliber AA defending their target, with a Wildcat from VMO-251 being ditched. Note that this particular aircraft lacks its canopy and has upper fuselage damage. The tailhook has also been extended. (NARA)

The US Navy's emphasis on deflection shooting was a cornerstone to the success of the Wildcat at Guadalcanal. Trying to latch onto the tail of a Sui-sen risked a low energy and turning contest where the floatplane fighter held the de facto advantage. That was why US Marine Corps and US Navy Wildcat pilots honed their skillset to snap off bursts from any angle. Having guns of the same caliber also facilitated deflection shooting, compared with the Sui-sen's mixed armament of machine gun and cannon, with the latter being nigh impossible to aim in a turning fight. Furthermore, the two weapons were separate entities with different muzzle velocities and rates of fire. Such a mixture made deflection shooting all the more problematical and, under some combat circumstances, unmanageable.

## F4F-4 ARMAMENT

The armament layout of the F4F-4 added an additional Browning M2 0.50-cal. machine gun to each outer wing compared with the F4F-3, giving this Wildcat variant a total of six weapons. With a rate of fire of between 750–850 rounds per minute, this meant an accurate one-second burst from all six guns could land about 40 rounds into the airframe of a Sui-sen airframe. Each gun accommodated 240 rounds per weapon, compared with 450 rounds for each of the four M2s in the F4F-3. Some Guadalcanal pilots, including high-scoring ace Capt Joe Foss, deactivated the outer guns so they could extend their total firing time, with the additional ammunition feeding the remaining four M2s.

# MARION E. CARL

Marion Eugene Carl was born on November 1, 1915 in Hubbard, Oregon. In 1938, he graduated with a Bachelor of Science degree in Mechanical Engineering from Oregon State College. That same year he resigned a US Army Reserve commission to accept an appointment as an aviation cadet in the US Marine Corps. He subsequently graduated as a US Marine Corps aviator with the rank of second lieutenant on December 1, 1939. Carl was awarded the Navy Cross following his participation in the Battle of Midway while serving as a captain with F4F-3-equipped VMF-221, leading attacks from Midway island against superior numbers of enemy aircraft.

Carl was subsequently posted to VMF-223, and on August 20, 1942, 19 F4F-4 Wildcats from the unit landed at Henderson Field to become the first US Marine Corps fighter squadron to be based there. Having flown in from the escort carrier USS *Long Island* (ACV-1), the unit was commanded by Maj John Smith and comprised a mixture of experienced and new pilots. VMF-224 arrived ten days later, followed by VF-5. With replacement pilots drawn from other US Marine Corps squadrons, these three units bore the brunt of Guadalcanal's air war until mid-October 1942.

Only four days after reaching Guadalcanal, VMF-224 intercepted a strike force of Nakajima B5N2 "Kate" torpedo-bombers, with fighter escort, from the carrier *Ryujo* that had been sent to attack Henderson Field during the Battle of the Eastern Solomons. Although three Wildcats were duly shot down, Carl claimed three torpedo-bombers and a Zero-sen, making him the first US Marine Corps ace – he had been credited with a Zero-sen shot down on June 4 during the defense of Midway.

Carl was awarded a Navy Cross during an early morning presentation service at Henderson Field on October 1, 1942. He received his medal from Adm Chester Nimitz, Commander-in-Chief US Pacific Fleet, who also decorated Carl's CO, Maj John Smith, and Maj Robert Galer, CO of VMF-224. All three had attained ace status by then, and were rightly recognized as the outstanding fighter pilots of the Guadalcanal campaign to date. Carl was eventually credited with downing 15.5 enemy aircraft during the battle for Guadalcanal, and by war's end he had claimed 18.5 kills.

In July 1943 Carl returned to Guadalcanal for his second tour of the Pacific, which also saw him serve in the New Hebrides, on Vella Lavella (again in the Solomons), and on Emirau Island. In November 1944 he was posted home from the Pacific, having earned three Distinguished Flying

Capt Marion Carl. (Author's Collection)

Crosses and 13 air medals. On V-J Day, he was promoted to lieutenant colonel.

In 1946, having been assigned to the Naval Air Test Center, Carl participated in the carrier deck trials of the Lockheed P-80 Shooting Star, and also became the first US Marine Corps helicopter pilot. In 1947 he earned his fourth Distinguished Flying Cross when he set a speed record in the Douglas Skystreak. He later commanded the first US Marine Corps jet fighter squadron, VMF-122, at MCAS Cherry Point, North Carolina, after which he formed the first jet aerobatic team. In 1953, while testing a high-altitude pressure suit, Carl set an altitude record in the US Navy's rocket-powered Douglas D-558-2 Skyrocket, earning him his fifth Distinguished Flying Cross.

In November 1954 he commanded photographic reconnaissance squadron VMJ-1 with the 1st Marine Aircraft Wing in Korea. In June 1955 Carl moved to Japan, where he was assigned as both Operations and Executive Officer of Marine Aircraft Group 11. Carl later joined the Division of Aviation at US Marine Corps Headquarters, and in July 1962 he was appointed Assistant Deputy Chief of Staff (Air). In July 1963 he served as Chief of Staff, 1st Marine Brigade, in Hawaii until January 1964, when he was promoted to brigadier general and appointed Commander of the Brigade. Carl later served in Vietnam, and his last military assignment was as Inspector General of the Marine Corps from July 1970 until May 1973. He retired on June 1, 1973, having undertaken just over 35 years of active service.

Tragically, Marion Carl lost his life on June 28, 1998 while protecting his wife during a home robbery in Roseburg, Oregon.

# SUI-SEN PILOT TRAINING

At the beginning of 1941, the IJNAF revised its pilot training syllabus and also commensurately increased graduate output. Thus it was that in the immediate period following the declaration of war, the IJNAF saw no need to further change its extant training regime. Until late 1941, pilot graduates undertook only limited operational training before assignment to a combat unit. This meant that when they arrived at forward units, pilots were usually assigned supernumerary roles so as to give them time to gain practical experience and area familiarization before being progressively immersed into operations.

The fundamentals of IJNAF aircrew training stemmed from its values, traditions and codes associated with being part of a navy, not an air force. The training focused on physical and skills superiority, with rigorous emphasis placed on physical fitness. Strict martial attitude was drilled into pilots during courses, all of whom had been taught in childhood that Japan had never lost a foreign war. This combination instilled students with utmost confidence in both themselves and the causes of Imperial Japan. The IJNAF initially anticipated, and thus planned for, a decisive war of limited duration, after which Japan would sue for peace. Its aircrew program set out to graduate high-quality pilots who would be part of a knock-out blow pending an armistice.

Contrary to Western stereotypes of Japanese fighting men as presented in post-war narratives and films, aircrew training also instilled willingness and aptitude to take initiative. The alleged mettle of the code of Bushido in World War II, often hailed in post-war Western literature as an embodiment of the samurai spirit, is mostly a myth. The IJNAF pilot was more a product of his training than this supposed and omnipresent Bushido code.

In the early interwar years, the IJNAF made extensive use of the locally designed and built Yokosuka Ro-go Type A floatplane. This example, one of 218 built between 1918 and 1924, is being lowered into the water from a seaplane tender. The IJN much admired the Royal Navy, emulating many of its operating procedures. (Author's Collection)

Nonetheless, honor was also emphasized as part of the training ethos, witnessed when genuine acts of jibaku (self-destruction) were sometimes seen by Allied pilots in the Solomons. In the case of Sui-sen pilots, this was evidenced when parachuting pilots released themselves from their harnesses high over water to ensure a quick death rather than enduring the shame of capture or to slowly perish from exposure.

When it came to providing pilots to fly the unique A6M2-N, the IJNAF was faced with a problem. The Sui-sen was very much a hybrid aircraft, and this meant it was going to be a challenge to find sufficient time and resources to convert extant floatplane pilots into fighter pilots, as was required by the Sui-sen's design. At least these aviators possessed a fundamental flying skillset, with many of them having acquired operational experience in the China theater. However, this does not obviate the case that most Sui-sen pilots had never flown a Zero-sen, which is what the A6M2-N essentially was.

The problems created by inexperienced pilots serving in Sui-sen units only worsened from late 1942 when attrition replacements started to arrive in the South Pacific, having just graduated from a truncated basic flying training course.

Yokosuka Kokutai was the key organization within the IJNAF for aviation engineering alongside the Naval Aviation Engineering Department. While the latter invented experimental aircraft and modifications, Yokosuka Kokutai had a key advisory role within the IJNAF, from which flowed considerable input into determining the training syllabus for Sui-sen pilots. Established in Oppama in April 1916, Yokosuka Kokutai enjoyed prestige from the fact it was the IJN's first naval air group. It became the operational unit tasked with pilot training, aviation research, and improvement of aircraft. With the rapid advancement of aviation during World War I, an airfield was built for Yokosuka Kokutai in Oppama in 1926.

An *ab initio* IJNAF training program was founded at Yokosuka in 1930, and two years later the Aviation Arsenal was established nearby. An overlooked part of pilot training was the reserves. In November 1934, the Air Reserve Student program was created, enabling university and college graduates to also enter the IJNAF pilot training scheme. Graduates were commissioned as ensigns, with officers from this program being distinguished from their academy counterparts through the designation "Reserve Officers," even in operational records. Although the reserve program was rather limited in terms of student numbers in the first few years, for some reason a disproportionate number of graduates wound up in Sui-sen units. The reserve program was appreciably expanded after the war situation worsened in 1943.

In the lead-up to the Pacific War, the three main floatplanes in operational units were the E8N2 "Dave," the F1M2 "Pete," and the E13A1 "Jake." Pilot training on the "Pete" also included aerial combat, so when the first A6M2-N was delivered to Yokosuka Kokutai, advanced pilot training was allocated to this unit. The Sui-sen's test pilot, Capt Ki'ichiro

A Type 93 Intermediate Training Aircraft (also known as the K5Y2 when equipped with floats) at the IJNAF training facility at Lake Kasumigaura. All Sui-sen pilots had initially trained on this type, Yokosuka building no fewer than 5,770 examples of the K5Y1 (with a fixed undercarriage), K5Y2, and K5Y3 (the latter two featured floats). (Author's Collection)

Nishihata, drew up a training program and became the main instructor on the type. During this time, his students gave him the sobriquet "*umi oya*" ("father of the seas").

Pre-war IJN flight training consisted of a seven-month *ab initio* course which advanced pilots to an intermediate level of flying skill. However, from commencement, flight training classes differentiated between landplanes and seaplanes. The syllabus for the latter type operated from the seaplane base and ramps alongside Lake Kasumigaura. Long-distance ocean navigation was taught as a critical skill, including the application of *de visu* ("by sight") drift methods. However, Sui-sen pilots also needed additional training and practice in maneuvers, gunnery, and a host of other fighter-related proficiencies. These skills were meant to be brought up to scratch and then enhanced within frontline units, but by late 1942 combat units had become short of replacement pilots.

Forward units sometimes conducted training exercises in combat zones. A good example occurred on January 18, 1943 when nine 802nd Kokutai Sui-sen undertook a series of training missions from Poporang Island. These involved towing cumbersome target sleeves, and a training flight of three was badly caught out by USAAF fighters that quickly shot down two of the Sui-sen.

IJN officers could be arrogant, and often reinforced their superiority to entrench a hierarchy which in some cases verged on a caste system. This elitist and internal factionalism also bred strong loyalties to one's particular training class, for both officer and non-officer alike. Thus, the Sui-sen pilots fighting in the South Seas from ships and harbor bases operated within this de facto caste system. Its effects were more often

An F1M2 "Petes" from *Kunikawa Maru* and four 802nd Kokutai Sui-sen are moored in the shallows off Poporang Island in early 1943. A6M2-Ns from this unit often "boomeranged" down to Rekata Bay from here, as the former location was too often threatened by raids from Allied aircraft, especially Wildcats. (Tony Holmes Collection)

than not diluted in a remote environment, and in the case of South Seas Sui-sen units, the system does not appear to have adversely impacted combat effectiveness or discipline.

Remarkably, Sui-sen pilots, like all IJNAF aviators assigned to operational units, were not given respite. They simply remained in the frontline until killed or wounded. Furthermore, they were aware that their American counterparts received regular leave. This caused a bitterness that quickly surfaced during the interrogations of captured IJNAF pilots, one of whom underlined that leaving pilots in combat without a break was "no way to run a war."

Without a break from the relentless stress of combat, the unyielding strain of facing death on a daily basis translated into a burden that weakened morale. IJNAF pilots who refused to fly due to combat fatigue could be threatened with a court-martial. However, in most cases, pilots unable to function due to stress were usually discreetly returned to Japan.

The average age of Sui-sen pilots entering the Solomons theater was on a par with their US counterparts – roughly 22 years old. The IJNAF rarely recognized good service to the individual, instead choosing to recognize the collective. Nonetheless, vigorous competition arose between pilots for the prestige of having the most battle success – a process through which morale was sometimes boosted.

The Sui-sen pilots who operated from Poporang and Faisi Islands came to regard the Shortlands as their South Seas home. Both pilots and support personnel were allowed to regularly write home, but they were not permitted to mention place names, nor the nature of their activities, in correspondence. Local villagers helped clean their camp and undertook chores in exchange for tinned food and other payments. Most of the younger and inexperienced pilots were keen to fly, for there was little else to do on base. Sui-sen unit commanders were amenable to giving such aviators an opportunity to fly via last-minute crew changes due to fatigue or illness.

Although there were short-wave radios on the island, no one was permitted to listen to Allied stations, and this ban was strictly enforced by officers. A daily news bulletin was printed, duplicated and distributed around the base, the contents of which were transmitted each morning by radio from Rabaul.

The floatplane anchorages were increasingly strafed by Allied aircraft returning from strike missions against southern Bougainville. Occasionally, a floatplane was damaged or destroyed by these raids, and less frequently support personnel were injured.

With malaria prevalent on Poporang Island, airmen were under strict orders to take quinine in an attempt to keep it at bay – a preventative exercise

Working for the *Asahi Shimbun* daily newspaper, Tomishige Yasuo was the principal civilian photographer assigned to the IJN in the South Seas theater throughout mid-1942. Seen here in standard IJNAF aircrew attire atop an H6K4 "Mavis" flying boat at Yokosuka naval base on March 4, 1942, Yasuo was, regrettably, absent from Rabaul when the Yokohama Kokutai's ten A6M2-Ns transited through there en route to Florida Island. (Author's Collection)

which proved reasonably successful. For the IJNAF, the forward bases in the Shortland Islands and on Poporang Island incubated diseases aside from malaria such as dengue fever. Widespread dysentery squandered pilot effectiveness, as did other deficiency disorders and tropical ailments, causing weight loss, muscular weakness, and skin lesions exacerbated by a lack of vitamins. Poor food quality (an issue for both the IJNAF and the US Navy/US Marine Corps alike) portended health issues and limited pilot effectiveness. The longer-term threat of tuberculosis also loomed. Badly wounded or seriously ill aircrew were evacuated to Buin or Rabaul for medical treatment on one of the regular H6K4 "Mavis" flights to the latter destination.

## A6M2-N ARMAMENT

The weaponry fitted in the Sui-sen emulated that of the A6M2 Zero-sen fighter on which the type's airframe was based. The floatplane fighter had a pair of 7.7mm Type 97 machine guns mounted in the upper fuselage just forward of the pilot that were synchronized to fire through the propeller. Each gun was belt-fed, with 500 rounds per weapon contained in an aluminum ammunition box. The Sui-sen also had a single 20 mm Type 99-1 cannon mounted in each mid-wing section. This was a comparatively light cannon with a low rate-of-fire of just nine rounds per second, and its effectiveness was further hampered by a low muzzle velocity. Each cannon was fed from a circular drum limited to 60 rounds per weapon.

## SUI-SAN UNIT TACTICS

The basic combat component in IJNAF fighter formations was the three- or four-aircraft flight (shotai), a variation of the V-formation consisting of a leader and two wingmen commonly employed by many air arms in World War II. However, Sui-sen pilots arrived in-theater with a major disadvantage. Unlike their Zero-sen counterparts, most of whom had already seen combat, the floatplane fighter pilots lacked similar experience and were not trained to the same level of proficiency in aerial combat as their land-based counterparts.

Both Zero-sen escort and combat tactics had been honed from the IJNAF's experiences in China, and passed down as folklore to fighter units. Such understandings were denied to Sui-sen pilots. As pilot losses took their toll, many A6M2-N replacements were posted to the Solomons from seaplane tenders, where they had flown more antiquated patrol floatplanes such as the E8N2 "Dave" or E13A1 "Jake." For these pilots their introduction to combat was a baptism of fire.

Furthermore, replacement Sui-sen pilots posted to combat units from late 1942 onwards often arrived in-theater having undertaken a truncated course of basic flight training. Surprisingly as it may seem, some had never even flown a Sui-sen. Equipped with little more than a cursory knowledge of floatplane flying, they lacked adequate gunnery and combat skills, not to mention familiarity with the fighter tactics required to succeed, let alone survive, in the Solomons. The assumption was that they would attain such skills once on operations. However, as the Sui-sen pilots became increasingly involved in patrols and aerial combat, there was less time available to undertake dedicated training missions to acquire such knowledge.

To be effective in fast-moving air combat with well-flown Wildcats, A6M2-N pilots required quick reactions, exceptional coordination, and an intuitive anticipation of the actions and reactions of their foe – attributes sorely lacking in the low-time replacements sent to the Solomons.

Adding to the woes of Sui-sen pilots, their bases in both the Shortland Islands and at Rekata Bay lacked an adequate early-warning capacity. Although the IJN established observation posts around the western coast of Guadalcanal, these were blind to Allied air movements headed north to Rekata Bay, or whose azimuth denied the accurate forecasting of their target destination. The posts in the Shortlands comprised little more than tree-top wooden platforms manned by ratings with binoculars. Observations made from such posts were often thwarted by cloud cover or oblique or circuitous approaches made by Allied aircraft to their target.

Basic maintenance facilities at airfields in the Solomons sometimes ensured a low Sui-sen serviceability rate, which in turn could limit patrols to only one or two shotai available for operations. Furthermore, insufficient floatplane fighters were available to maintain consistent patrols over bases, with enemy aircraft often arriving between them. With the approach of 1943, the ever-diminishing number of airworthy Sui-sen also saw them outnumbered in air combat, often badly so.

Yokohama Kokutai operated the first batch of production Sui-sen at Tulagi as a frontline experiment, largely with the objective of gaining useful data and intelligence on flying the type in a tropical environment in combat. The IJNAF had previously done this with the Zero-sen when the type was deployed to the China theater with

12th Kokutai in the summer of 1940, and it was analogous to the way the Imperial Japanese Army Air Force's 47th Independent Chutai had introduced the Nakajima Ki-44 Shoki to frontline operations in Indochina in December 1941. Initial evaluation of Sui-sen performance in-theater was thwarted when those most able and qualified to impart lessons learned were killed in the strafing attacks on the Halavo Bay and Gavutu Island bases on August 7, 1942.

While on patrol, Sui-sen pilots loosened their V-formations to take account of the larger size of their fighters, with wingmen lagging further back and at different altitudes, instead of being tied closely to the leader. These revised formations saw typical, but staggered, distances of around 200–300m behind the leader, giving the wingmen more time and scope to scan the sky for enemy aircraft without concerning themselves about mid-air collision. Ground attacks were often made in line abreast, as the tactical situation required.

The Sui-sen had one obvious advantage compared with the Zero-sen. If engine power was lost or an airframe damaged, the floatplane fighter could be put down on water. Its pilot would then wait to be rescued, either by a comrade in another floatplane or by a friendly ship – this happened several times. Zero-sen pilots, on the other hand, always lost their mounts when they ditched, meaning rescue was a more hazardous proposition, if attempted at all.

A decline in Zero-sen strength at Buin was briefly offset by bolstering the reconstituted 14th Kokutai when it was recast as 802nd Kokutai on November 1, 1942. This unit often "boomeranged" its Sui-sen down to Rekata Bay from the Shortlands, as the former location was too often threatened by raids from Allied aircraft, especially Wildcats.

The predominant floatplane types operating alongside the Sui-sen were the F1M2 "Pete," used for observation, and the E13A1 "Jake" reconnaissance aircraft, supplemented by several older model floatplanes used for liaison including the E8N2 "Dave" biplane. Nocturnal operations included armed reconnaissance and bombing

The main floatplane anchorage at Malaguna in Rabaul's Simpson Harbor was the Sui-sens' first home in the South Seas theater. They had long gone by the time this photograph of E13A1 "Jakes" of 958th Kokutai was taken there in mid-1943. (Author's Collection)

# A6M2-N SUI-SEN COCKPIT

1. IJNAF Type 98 reflector gunsight
2. Artificial horizon
3. Turn-and-bank indicator
4. Compass
5. IJNAF Type 97 7.7mm machine guns
6. Rate-of-climb indicator
7. Fuel pressure gauge
8. Tachometer
9. Cylinder head temperature gauge
10. Oil temperature gauge
11. Intake manifold pressure gauge
12. Oil cooler shutter handle
13. Ignition plug charger switch
14. Rudder bar
15. Oxygen control box
16. Oxygen pressure gauge
17. Oxygen quantity gauge
18. Control column
19. Wing fuel tank quantity gauge
20. Fuselage fuel tank quantity gauge
21. Switchboard
22. Fuel injection pump
23. Engine main switch
24. Radio direction indicator
25. Altimeter
26. Exhaust temperature gauge
27. Clock
28. Airspeed indicator
29. Interior lights
30. Radio homing control unit
31. Type 3 Mark 1 radio control panel
32. Arresting hook retraction handle
33. Arresting hook/flap down angle indicator
34. Radio homing equipment control lever
35. Cowl gills control handle
36. Cockpit ventilation air intake
37. Pilot's seat adjustment lever
38. Pilot's seat
39. Elevator trim tab control handle
40. Machine gun safety lever
41. Throttle lever
42. Machine gun selector switch
43. Propeller pitch adjustment lever
44. Mixture control lever
45. Drop tank release lever
46. Bomb release levers
47. Switchboard
48. Flap control handle
49. Fuselage/wing tank switching cock
50. Wing tanks selector switches
51. High-altitude automatic mixture control
52. Wing tanks selector lever

missions, neither of which inflicted major damage. These missions, however, could significantly restrict PT boat operations by forcing them to cut their speed in order to reduce highly visible wakes whenever floatplanes lurked overhead – such missions were more often conducted by the slower, two-seat F1M2 "Pete."

As previously noted, the Sui-sen's 20mm cannon was almost impossible to aim properly when the fighter was engaged in aerobatic maneuvers in combat mainly due to its low rate-of-fire. Landing sufficient shells into an F4F-4 to damage it, let alone bring it down, when maneuvering proved unachievable for most pilots. An experienced marksmen also required good luck, or fleetingly being positioned in the right place at the right time.

Compared with its A6M2 derivative, the Sui-sen was saddled with increased weight and aerodynamic drag caused by the main float and pylon. Given these hindrances, its pilots nevertheless used its admirable maneuverability to their advantage, despite an overall decrease in both general and combat performance of about 20 percent compared with the Zero-sen. The Sui-sen was operated in the South Pacific in a defensive role, rather than the offensive one specified by the IJNAF when it issued the 15-Shi specification in 1940.

The frequent non-performance of Sui-sen radios often led to a complete lack of communication, thus limiting tactical control usually exercised by flight leaders. This unhappy situation arose because of the factory-installed Type 96 voice/telegraph radio equipment fitted into the airframe. Transmitting in the frequency range 3.8–5.8 megahertz (the lower end of the high frequency band), the radio consisted of three components, all installed in the fuselage. Transmitter and receiver comprised separate units positioned low on the right side of the cockpit, hung in a shock mount provided via bungee cords – a simple but effective protector. Separately, a dynamotor that powered the radio was mounted on a shelf to the left rear behind the pilot's elbow.

Although the radio sets were well-designed and well-built, their performance in the tropics was hindered by poor shielding and grounding of the installation. The deficient shielding of the Sui-sen engine's dual ignition system in particular badly interfered with radio reception and transmission – the same problem affected the radio fitted in the A6M2 Zero-sen. Static charges were also generated by movement of the airframe through the humid atmosphere. There were few IJNAF technicians in the South Seas sufficiently familiar with the radio system to effectively modify let alone maintain them, try as they might. Gigantean cumulonimbus cloud formations that built up over the Solomons Sea were also excellent generators of atmospheric static, further degrading radio reception at all altitudes.

The usual problems of serviceability at forward bases attended the Sui-sen. By early November 1942, the number of airworthy floatplane airframes in the Shortlands was considerably reduced, with just half of the aircraft present being serviceable at any one time. The ability to carry out repairs following combat damage and the replacement of worn out parts was slowed by the fact that several key seaplane tenders had been tasked with undertaking other more pressing roles, including acting as general transports. These tenders had provided, inter alia, protected engineering facilities and a ready source of spare parts. The sidelining of these ships meant less direct support for the R-Area Force units, including those supporting Sui-sen, and restricted the IJN's capacity for shipping replacement A6M2-Ns from Japan.

# RI'ICHIRO SATO

Ri'ichiro Sato was born in Okegawa, Japan, a satellite town to the northwest of Tokyo. Graduating from Class 66 at Eta Jima Naval Academy in 1938, he learned to fly on the Yokosuka Type 93 Intermediate Training Aircraft (also known as the K5Y2 when equipped with floats) at the seaplane training base at Lake Kasumigaura. Appointed to lead the Yokohama Kokutai on May 15, 1942, Sato subsequently led a detachment known as the "Hama" Kokutai to the South Seas theater following its creation in Japan on April 1, 1942.

The Sui-sen detachment was shipped to Rabaul on June 3, 1942 with an allocation of 12 A6M2-N Sui-sen and four spares as deck cargo. The detachment moored its new floatplane fighters at Malaguna Beach, christened the Maruki floatplane base, in Simpson Harbor. On June 6, 13 Sui-sen led by Sato made a three-and-a-half hour patrol around Rabaul and the Gazelle Peninsula that constituted the type's first flight in the South Seas theater. A repeat patrol was led by Sato the following day, this time involving all 16 assembled and tested Sui-sen. The detachment experienced its first aerial combat on June 10 when five Sui-sen unsuccessfully, and fleetingly, engaged B-26s from the 22nd Bombardment Group (BG) as they fled after making a low-level attack on Rabaul's main wharf area.

The "Hama" Kokutai pilots ferried themselves to their new base at Halavo Bay on Florida Island in separate flights in early July. From here, Sato led the first patrol of the Guadalcanal/Tulagi area on July 5. The Tulagi area detachment comprised 36 engineers/groundcrew and 12 pilots. The following day, Sato led the Sui-sen's first combat mission from the new base, engaging a B-17E sent to reconnoitre both Tulagi and Guadalcanal.

The first month at Halavo Bay was relatively comfortable. Both Sato and his Executive Officer, WO Tokuchiyo Hirahashi, were photography aficionados, and they were often seen capturing images of Tulagi and its environs with their Zeiss-Ikon folding cameras. On some evenings officers from the detachment took a launch from Halavo across the bay to the former Tulagi British colonial club on a hill overlooking the town which the IJN had converted into their own officers' club. Meanwhile, Sato would lead nearly all missions, including a six Sui-sen patrol on July 17 in which they intercepted and downed a solitary 435th BS B-17E. During this mission, FPO1c Tatsuo Hori was shot down and killed, marking the detachment's first combat loss.

Meanwhile, Sato wrote numerous field reports that were dispatched to Yokosuka Kokutai headquarters in Japan, describing the technical challenges and performance of the Sui-sen under frontline and combat conditions. These reports were also copied to the Naval Aviation Engineering Department in Tokyo and the aircraft's manufacturer, Nakajima. They were couriered to Japan on the regular Rabaul–Tokyo route operated by IJN Combined Fleet H6K4 "Mavis" flying boats.

Ri'ichiro Sato. (Author's Collection)

At dawn on August 7, VF-71 Wildcats destroyed most of the unit's inventory and base facilities when they strafed Halavo Bay floatplane base and the slipways on the nearby twin islets of Gavutu and Tanambogo. This was the opening surprise attack for the amphibious invasion of Tulagi launched by the US Marine Corps a few hours later. Only two or three "Hama" Kokutai detachment Sui-sen, then briefly visiting the Shortland Islands, survived the strike.

Unable to get away, many of the detachment's pilots and groundcrew fled inland to the mountains on Florida Island behind the base. Here, they were later hunted down and killed by US Marine Corps patrols over the next few weeks. It was during one of these raids in late August 1942 that Sato was killed. Unit personnel captured on Florida Island were later sent to New Zealand, where, under interrogation as PoWs, they provided much detail about the detachment's early days.

Sato, the first Sui-sen combat leader, led "Hama" Kokutai from the front and flew whenever he could. His field reports influenced the deployment and training of future A6M2-N pilots that were sent to units in the South Seas and other theaters.

# COMBAT

Two F4F-4s from VF-71 are readied for their next mission on the flightdeck of *Wasp* on August 7, 1942, these aircraft having already wrought devastation on the Sui-sen of Yokohama Kokutai at Tulagi earlier that day. The *Wasp*'s SBDs and TBFs chained down behind them would also see plenty of action during operations in-theater on the 7th. (Public Domain)

In the South Seas theater, the Sui-sen was operated by both shore- and ship-based units. In practice, this led to two main outcomes. First, Sui-sen routinely flew with other types of floatplanes, mainly the F1M2 "Pete," and second, an overall shortage of floatplanes saw units often conduct combined operations. However, the first Sui-sen versus Wildcat contest was a one-sided affair that saw no actual aerial combat. Rather, a surprise low-level strafing attack all but wiped out the first Sui-sen unit committed to frontline operations.

In June 1942, Yokohama Kokutai formed a fighter wing equipped with Sui-sen. Led by Lt Cdr Soichi Tashiro, with Lt Cdr Yoshijiro Suzuki as hikotaicho (commander of all flight personnel), the wing soon became colloquially known as the "Hama Kokutai." It arrived at Rabaul that same month with 16 Sui-sen – 12 operational floatplane fighters and four reserves, allocated tail numbers in the block Y-151 to Y-166. When this unit was called forward to the Solomons in July, it commenced patrols of the area and successfully attacked Espirito Santo-based B-17Es targeting Tulagi and Guadalcanal.

After an early breakfast at 0345 hrs aboard the carrier *Wasp* on August 7, 1942, aircraft were launched in darkness as part of the US Marine Corps' amphibious invasion of Tulagi and

Guadalcanal. The combination of a barely discernible horizon and three US Navy carriers in close proximity prompted pilots to view the coming launch with some trepidation. Due to the challenging circumstances, VF-71 CO Lt Cdr Courtney Shands was only able to assemble 11 of 16 Wildcats that took off from *Wasp*. Once the pilots had launched, visibility improved thanks to moonlight illuminating the cloudless sky. Shands' formation was the first to reach the Tulagi area, including the twin islets of Gavutu and Tanambogo, and Halavo Bay.

Shands set up his Wildcats in a low-level sweep of the target, and he immediately recognized floatplanes and flying boats as they approached Tulagi. When his Wildcats arrived at 0615 hrs, with sunrise still some 16 minutes away, the Yokohama Kokutai had just completed refueling and arming its Sui-sen in preparation for a morning patrol. Launches and fuel barges scurried between shore, anchored vessels, and floatplanes. Shands and wingman Ens Samuel Forrer spotted six Sui-sen moored line abreast offshore Halavo village beach on Florida Island, a mile east of the Gavutu/Tanambogo complex. The floatplane fighters presented themselves as "ducks" in a shooting gallery, allowing both pilots to set all six Sui-sen alight as they raked them with their 0.50-cal. machine guns – the latter had incendiary rounds interspersed amongst standard armor-piercing bullets.

Meanwhile, other VF-71 Wildcats had found two more "Rufes" on one of Tanambogo's slipways, and these too were destroyed. Later reports indicated that a single "Float Zero" was seen to take-off during the attack. This was possible, as two or three Sui-sen survived this attack, at least one of which had flown to the Shortland Islands in previous days on liaison duties.

Another pair of Wildcats led by Lt Spencer Wright found four fully-fueled "Mavis" flying boats moored off the northern tip of Tanambogo, allowing Wright to set them on fire. They all sank at their moorings shortly thereafter.

Having destroyed the Sui-sen offshore Halavo village beach, Shands and Forrer headed toward another mooring zone at nearby Makambo Island, where they strafed and destroyed two more H6K4 "Mavis" flying boats. A third example, seen taxiing for take-off, was targeted by another pair of Wildcats, and it too was destroyed. The surprise attack had effectively wiped out the floatplane fighter element of the Yokohama Kokutai, and destroyed seven of its equally valuable H6K4s. Several personnel were killed aboard the flying boats, with more casualties incurred amongst those onboard the launches and barges that were also strafed by the Wildcats.

The unexpected invasion of Tulagi and Guadalcanal presented 11th Air Fleet at Rabaul with a number of unprecedented challenges, among which was how to make good the loss of the Sui-sen detachment. The answer came in the form of the A6M2-N ship-borne unit attached to the seaplane tender *Kamikawa Maru*. Its air

This aerial reconnaissance photograph taken during a low-level pass by a USAAF aircraft over Gavutu Island reveals the remains of Sui-sen constructor number 821, destroyed near the slipway on August 7, 1942 by F4F-4s from VF-71. A detached main float and pylon lay in front of the derelict airframe. (Author's Collection)

A *Kamikawa Maru* Sui-sen, to the left, and a pair of F1M2 "Petes" from the same seaplane tender were moored off the Shortland Islands when this photograph was taken in September 1942. On the 14th of that month, no fewer than three *Kamikawa Maru* A6M2-Ns were lost to Wildcats over Henderson Field. (Author's Collection)

wing had been supervised by hikotaicho Lt Cdr Tsunemaru Eto when the vessel first arrived in the South Seas theater in April 1942. On May 2, its "Dave" and "Pete" floatplanes started using Rekata Bay for the first time when they stationed themselves overnight there to cover the Japanese occupation of Tulagi. Although *Kamikawa Maru*'s inventory lacked Sui-sen at this early stage in the South Seas campaign, its pilots nevertheless gained valuable operational experience in this alien theater.

Then in July 1942 *Kamikawa Maru* was unexpectedly reassigned to the distant Aleutians, not returning to Poporang Island in the Shortlands until September, when it delivered 11 Sui-sen (red tail codes YII-101 to YII-111), along with two "Petes" (red tail codes YII-1 and YII-3). After being offloaded, the Sui-sen were structured into two-aircraft shotai in order to fulfil reconnaissance and defense roles. The 11-strong pilot cadre was led by buntaicho (division commander) Lt Jiro Ono. The vessel's Sui-sen were thus the first to replace the "Hama Kokutai" destroyed at Tulagi on August 7.

During the late afternoon of September 13, A6M2-N pilots FCPO Jiro Kawai and WO Makio Kawamura shot down an SBD Dauntless from VMSB-231 overhead Henderson Field as it returned from a solo patrol. These pilots were part of a *Kamikawa Maru* detachment that had been based temporarily at Rekata Bay to reconnoiter the ongoing land campaign to retake Henderson Field. The downing of the SBD was also the first time Sui-sen had acted offensively by seeking out enemy aircraft, rather than defending IJN facilities from attack by USAAF bombers.

After overnighting at Rekata Bay, buntaicho FCPO Jiro Kawai set off on a solo patrol in his Sui-sen at dawn on September 14 to ascertain whether the IJA had managed to successfully occupy the airfield. Flying over Lunga Point, he observed nothing conclusive. The major Japanese ground assault to retake Henderson Field had in fact been halted at around 0900 hrs. Four more *Kamikawa Maru* Sui-sen led by Lt(jg) Masashi Kawashima subsequently took off on a follow-up reconnaissance mission of the American-held airfield, which they overflew at an altitude of just 900 m at 0930 hrs. The floatplane fighters initially circled the base, before one pilot was distracted by a departing R4D transport aircraft.

Forewarned of the presence of four IJN aircraft approaching Henderson Field, 11 F4F-4s from VF-5 were scrambled in response to the alert. With the advantage of altitude, the Wildcat pilots shot down the Sui-sen flown by Kawashima and wingmen FPO1c Toshio Oyama and WO Makio Kawamura.

This was an instructive engagement, for it was the first time the two types had met in aerial combat. The incumbent VF-5 Wildcat pilots involved duly submitted detailed combat reports. Unit CO Lt Cdr Leroy Simpler, with Lt Walter Clarke as his wingman, had led the Wildcats into the attack. Clarke had banked to port and followed Simpler down when he broke away from the VF-5 formation to chase a Sui-sen trying to flee at wavetop height. When the floatplane fighter suddenly pulled up in a wingover, Clarke gave it a three-second burst just before the Sui-sen levelled off overland. Another burst at close range saw only two of the Wildcat's six guns fire. Nevertheless, Clarke's quarry started smoking, before it dived into the ground and burst into flames.

Lt(jg) Frank Green had his electrical system shot out during a head-on pass with a "Rufe." He submitted that he was sure he had hit his attacker before two more Wildcats jumped the same Sui-sen, "flaming" the floatplane and sending it down. Lt(jg) Elisha Stover was following another Sui-sen when it was suddenly attacked by other Wildcats. The Sui-sen made a violent Immelmann turn in an attempt to escape, almost hitting a startled Stover in the process. The US Navy pilot nonetheless continued to follow it until his guns jammed about 50ft from the Sui-sen's tail, whereupon Stover broke off his attack. By then his opponent's cockpit was both "shattered" and "smoking."

Lt(jg) Howard Grimmell followed another Sui-sen out to sea toward Tulagi, firing at the floatplane with repeated bursts, but he was frustrated when it failed to turn to offer him a "bigger target." Although Grimmell found that none of his bursts had had any apparent effect on the aircraft, the Sui-sen was soon downed by other Wildcats.

Ens John Wesolowski dove on the first of the four Sui-sen to be encountered, swinging in behind it for a stern pass. However, his opponent possessed sufficient maneuverability to reverse his course of flight and confront Wesolowski head-on. The American returned fire as the floatplane fighter flashed past overhead, before again turning sharply.

Ens George Morgan fired at another Sui-sen at close range and it exploded in his face – heat from the fireball created by the A6M2-N could be felt through the windscreen. However, it was Ens James Halford who had had the most dramatic encounter. He attacked the leading Sui-sen – likely the aircraft flown by Lt(jg) Masashi Kawashima – and it banked sharply to starboard. Halford managed to turn inside the floatplane, before diving after it and latching onto its tail, firing as he did. As the Sui-sen fell away in flames, the pilot bailed out and his parachute opened. Revealing the brutal nature of the fighting in the Solomons, Halford then made two gunnery runs at the descending pilot, reporting that he was sure he had killed him.

Having returned to Rekata Bay, the sole surviving pilot of the quartet sent out on the mission conveyed the news that three of his comrades had been lost and Henderson Field was most definitely still in American hands. Accordingly, a substantial R-Area Force strike was organized, with floatplanes departing the Shortland Islands at 1300 hrs to stage through Rekata Bay prior to attacking Henderson Field.

The force was comprised of 19 F1M2 floatplanes led by the *Chitose* air detachment buntaicho, Lt Takeshi Horibata, with each "Pete" toting a pair of 60kg bombs. These aircraft were a conglomerate drawn from the air detachments of the seaplane tenders *Chitose* (eight), *Sanyo Maru* (four), *Sanuki Maru* (five), and *Kamikawa Maru* (two). Horibata devised a sneak attack designed to approach the target from Guadalcanal's west coast, before swinging inland to hit Henderson from the south. With sunset at 1817 hrs, he anticipated a dusk approach that would further surprise the Americans.

Separately, in order to cover the attacking "Petes," a pair of *Kamikawa Maru* Sui-sen led by buntaicho Lt Jiro Ono would cruise well above the strike force at 2,400m, hoping to ward off interfering Wildcats. The combined formation departed Rekata Bay just after 1600 hrs, expecting to catch parked aircraft at Henderson Field. However, Horibata's floatplane formation was detected by radar as it approached over the ocean, obviating the element of surprise and allowing the scramble at 1745 hrs of a combined formation of 11 Wildcats from VF-5 and VMF-224.

Lt(jg) Elisha Stover shot down the *Kamikawa Maru* Sui-sen flown by Flyer1c Matsutaro Omura during the "Pete" floatplane attack on Henderson Field in the late afternoon of September 14, 1942. A veteran of the Battle of Midway, Stover would later lose his life after being shot down over Truk while flying an F6F-3 Hellcat of VF-5 from USS *Yorktown* (CV-10) on February 16, 1944. He was one of seven US Navy aircrew beheaded with swords following their capture by the IJN. (Tony Holmes Collection)

The five aircraft from the latter unit, led by Maj John Dobbin and his wingman Lt George Hollowell, engaged the "Petes" first as the floatplanes descended over Guadalcanal's mountains to the south before heading in the direction of the airfield. Dobbin and Hollowell tore into the F1M2s, achieving complete surprise and scattering the formation. Two (one each from *Chitose* and *Sanyo Maru*) fell after this first attack. Shortly thereafter, a *Kamikawa Maru* Sui-sen flown by Flyer1c Matsutaro Omura was separately engaged by Lt(jg) Elisha Stover, who later reported:

> [I] came down and met two Zeros, float type, at 8,000ft SW of island. I got into a dogfight that gave me an almost full deflection shot at one as he pulled into a wingover in front of me. He started flaming and crashed into mountains. The other broke off and headed west at high speed.

When flames burst from his Sui-sen, Omura jumped out of it over Mt Austin but his parachute failed to deploy and he fell to his death. Although proximate to a Japanese-held area, his body was not recovered by IJA forces too pre-occupied with their own survival. Following his narrow escape, buntaicho FCPO Jiro Ono fled in his Sui-sen back to Rekata Bay, where he reported Omura's loss and described the strike by the "Petes" as successful.

## BOUGAINVILLE STRIKE

Meanwhile, in the midst of the Guadalcanal land campaign, the US Navy decided to conduct a series of carrier strikes against airfields in Bougainville. These were undertaken on October 5 by aircraft from *Hornet*, with the Shortlands being amongst several targets hit because of its role as a major seaplane base. The carrier had approached to an area south of the Shortlands on the evening of the 4th, intent on striking both the base and warships anchored in nearby Tonolei Harbor.

These P-400 Airacobras of the 67th FS have been parked close together at Henderson Field after completing a mission in late 1942. The Wildcat sometimes found itself fighting alongside, or escorting, Airacobras in this timeframe. Sui-sen and other IJNAF floatplanes were also very occasionally engaged by Airacobras. (Author's Collection)

Early on the morning of 5 October, 16 F4F-4s from VF-72 launched first, their pilots having been tasked with protecting the bombers from the carrier air group. Once the targets had been attacked, the Wildcat pilots could conduct their own strafing passes.

The weather for the entire day was poor, with squalls and thunderstorms badly limiting visibility. The Wildcats were overhead the Shortlands just after dawn at 0610 hrs, and they quickly set about strafing around 20 "float Zeros" moored along the beach. They also found larger "Mavis" flying boats, claiming three damaged. When they initially reached the target area, two Sui-sen were already aloft on CAP, and they were joined by three more that had scrambled. Sporadic aerial combat ensued between cloudbanks and the rain, and despite claims from both sides, no aircraft were lost in a series of cat-and-mouse engagements. Several of the moored Sui-sen were damaged by the strafing, however. The attack underlined what the IJNAF had known all along – any coastal seaplane base offered only a limited area in which to try and disperse floatplanes.

Wildcats confronted Sui-sen once again on October 10 when, at dawn, a strike force of 15 SBDs and six TBFs took off from Henderson Field to attack another incoming "Tokyo Express" destroyer supply run. Fighter escort was provided by eight USAAF P-39s and 15 Wildcats from VMF-223 and VMF-224. The Japanese warships were found at 0640 hrs in clear conditions, and the SBDs began their diving attacks from 9,000ft, while the Wildcats strafed their hulls as TBFs made their torpedo runs.

R-Area Force had provided two *Kamikawa Maru* Sui-sen and two *Sanuki Maru* "Petes" to cover the destroyers. As the Wildcats strafed the ships, the floatplanes tried to intervene from above. Subsequent combat saw all four overwhelmed and shot down, Sui-sen pilots FCPO Jiro Kawai (in YII-104) and Flyer1c Shinichi Maruyama (in YII-107) both being killed. The only American loss was the 339th Fighter Squadron (FS) Airacobra flown by 2Lt Karl Banfield, although whether he was downed by a floatplane or AA fire from one of the destroyers is unclear.

Shortly thereafter, recent Sui-sen losses were made good by the arrival of 14th Kokutai. This unit had initially been commissioned to serve in the China theater pre-war, only to be deactivated on September 15, 1941. Reactivated on April 19, 1942 at Yokosuka under the command of Cdr Daizo Nakajima, its primary role was to both

Wildcat pilots rest near, and within, "The Pagoda," which had been abandoned by the Japanese following the US capture of Henderson Field. It briefly served as the headquarters of the 1st Marine Air Wing, the sign overhead the entrance proudly stating *HENDERSON FIELD – US MARINE CORPS*. A solitary Wildcat can just be seen in the landing pattern above the wooden structure. (Author's Collection)

trial and operate the new H8K1 "Emily" flying boat from Rabaul. A fighter wing was established at Yokosuka on September 20, 1942, with the unit's ten pilots being led by buntaicho Lt Hideo Goto and deputy Lt(jg) Toshio Igarashi.

Eleven Sui-sen from 14th Kokutai were loaded aboard *Kiyokawa Maru* as deck cargo on October 2. Two of the floatplane fighters were damaged nine days later when the ship was bombed by an RAAF Hudson as it approached Rabaul. The nine remaining airworthy Sui-sen were offloaded at Malaguna, in Rabaul's Simpson Harbor, after which 14th Kokutai pilots ferried them to Poporang Island. A tenth followed a few days later after the damage it had suffered during the Hudson attack had been repaired. A week later, the bulk of the unit's engineers and more support crew were delivered to Poporang Island by "Mavis" flying boat, the personnel being led by chief engineer Lt Seita Miyake. The Sui-sen from 14th Kokutai now joined their *Kamikawa Maru* counterparts in conducting joint operations and patrols from the Shortlands, often staging through Rekata Bay.

Meanwhile, other 14th Kokutai Sui-sen had joined the *Kamikawa Maru* detachment at Rekata Bay, from where they challenged SBDs conducting dawn raids against the seaplane base. During the late afternoon of October 17, for example, four A6M2-Ns of 14th Kokutai engaged and shot down an SBD from VS-71, with FPO2c Hisao Chiryou receiving credit for the kill. However, when returning from this mission at dusk, FPO2c Minoru Okuyama misjudged his landing flare at Rekata Bay in the darkness, overturning his Sui-sen. Badly injured in the crash, Okuyama was evacuated to Rabaul the following day by "Mavis" flying boat.

The next major Sui-sen engagement with Wildcats occurred on October 30. The previous afternoon, a mixed formation of 12 floatplanes had flown into Rekata Bay from Poporang Island prior to undertaking escort missions the following day for the IJN destroyers *Shigure* and *Ariake* returning to Tonolei Harbor from an overnight supply run to Guadalcanal. For this operation, three 14th Kokutai Sui-sen were joined by an example from *Kamikawa Maru*, and they would in turn sortie with eight "Petes."

Parked beneath palm trees at Turtle Bay airfield on Espiritu Santo, four F4F-3s of VMO-251 await fueling and servicing in November 1942. The last unit in the Solomons equipped with four-gun Wildcats, VMO-251 strafed floatplane bases and engaged Sui-sen in aerial combat whilst flying from Henderson Field. (Tony Holmes Collection)

The floatplanes' arrival at Rekata Bay had been reported by a Coastwatcher to Guadalcanal, and at dawn on the 30th, seven F4F-3/4s from VMO-251 and VMF-212 were led aloft by 1Lt Jack Conger. They planned to arrive overhead the IJNAF base just before sunrise and conduct a surprise strike. Guided to the target by kerosene lamps scattered throughout the Japanese camp, the Wildcats found 12 floatplanes in the throes of departure. The four Sui-sen at Rekata Bay were attempting to take off when the Wildcats struck. Superior Flyer Teruo Watanabe was quickly shot down, his Sui-sen breaking apart as it hit the water – he survived, however.

Lt Hideo Goto was leading the quartet of A6M2-Ns, and although he managed to get airborne, his aircraft had been so badly shot up that he abandoned the escort mission and instead fled back to the Shortlands. There, his Sui-sen was subsequently written off. Masked by poor visibility and low light conditions, fellow pilots FPO1c Eiji Matsuyama, flying W-107, and FPO2c Hisao Jitou briefly fought the Wildcats before also disappearing toward the Shortlands. Jitou claimed two Wildcats destroyed (none were in fact lost), and he arrived in the Shortlands shortly after Goto. His main float had been badly holed by the Wildcats, causing the Sui-sen to sink in shallow water upon landing.

In this early morning fracas the shot-up Sui-sen were followed aloft by six "Petes," one of which was downed, badly injuring *Sanyo Maru* observer FPO1c Keizou Furudera – he died four days later. Watanabe's Sui-sen and the *Sanyo Maru* "Pete" were the only two direct combat losses, despite the generous five confirmed aerial victories awarded to the Wildcat pilots. Three more floatplanes were claimed destroyed on the beach when the Wildcats strafed the base extensively before returning to Guadalcanal. Such claims remain doubtful, however, as the Japanese were masters of consistently positioning already-damaged airframes as decoys along the bay's shoreline.

Later that same day, three more 14th Kokutai Sui-sen conducted another protective convoy mission from Rekata Bay, before returning early the next morning to the safety of Poporang Island. This proved to be the final flight of 14th Kokutai before it was redesignated 802nd Kokutai on November 1 as part of an IJNAF-wide unit restructure.

A *Sanyo Maru* F1M2 "Pete" floatplane abandoned at Rekata Bay. The IJNAF regularly moved such hulks around as decoys, leading to hyper-inflated US claims for the number of floatplanes destroyed from strafing attacks in the Solomons. (Author's Collection)

The creation of 802nd at Poporang Island was essentially an administrative exercise, with no change in operational or command structures.

A week later, on November 7, buntaicho Lt Hideo Goto led five Sui-sen in a mixed formation with an A6M2-N and two "Petes" from *Kamikawa Maru* to cover a sizeable "Tokyo Express" convoy comprising 11 destroyers on a supply run to Guadalcanal. The aircraft were intercepted during the late afternoon by 16 Wildcats (from VMF-112 and VMF-121) and eight Airacobras, which were escorting SBDs and TBFs en route to attack the destroyers. The weather was cloudy, interspersed with bands of rain – ideal conditions for a successful surprise attack, as the American pilots duly proved by downing all six Sui-sen and a "Pete" from *Kamikawa Maru*.

The eight floatplanes had departed the Shortlands shortly after 1400 hrs. Aware of the destroyers' presence, the Cactus Air Force had organized a substantial air strike in an attempt to thwart their passage through "The Slot." Flying top cover for the SBDs and torpedo-armed TBFs tasked with attacking the destroyers were eight Wildcats from VMF-121 led by Capt Joe Foss and an identical number from VMF-112 led by unit CO, Maj Paul Fontana. Eight P-39 Airacobras from the 339th FS, each armed with a 500lb bomb, also headed for the IJN vessels. However, the fighter-bombers, led by Capt John Mitchell, became separated from the Wildcats by the weather and arrived slightly later.

At 1615 hrs, 2Lt William Hronek, flying an SBD from VMSB-132 on a separate afternoon search mission for the destroyers, was attacked by two "Petes" and four Sui-sen from the floatplane escort as they defended the convoy off Choiseul's southern

tip. The floatplanes were driven off by Hronek's rear gunner, who claimed a "Zero" destroyed. During the course of their attack, the IJNAF pilots failed to spot the Wildcats overhead. Taking full advantage of their superior height, the American pilots made a masterful "hit and run" pass on their unwary opponents north of Vangunu Island, 150 miles northwest of Henderson Field.

Capt Joe Foss, the Executive Officer of VMF-121, led the attack with his eight Wildcats, joined shortly thereafter by the Airacobras, whose pilots jettisoned their bombs prior to diving into the melee. They quickly engaged the floatplanes that had survived the devastating pass made by VMF-121, claiming five shot down. Given the circumstances, the combat was decisive, with all six Sui-sen being destroyed. It appears that two of the floatplane fighters survived the initial bounce, only to then be downed in a series of scattered dogfights with the P-39s that ensued.

The *Kamikawa Maru* Sui-sen pilot lost in this action was WO Hisateru Kofuji, one of the few survivors of the Yokohama Kokutai detachment wiped out at Tulagi in August. The five 802nd Kokutai Sui-sen downed were flown by Lt Hideo Goto, FPO2c Hisao Jitou (flying W-107, whose original 14th Kokutai tail code had not yet been updated), FPO3c Jirou Kondo, FPO2c Sadatoku Hagiwara, and Superior Flyer Hajime Mizokuchi.

Having broken away from combat following a series of passes that subsequently saw him claim a "Float Zero" and two "float biplanes" destroyed, Capt Foss was confused by the sight of five parachutes deployed but without anyone hanging beneath them. He then saw a sixth Japanese pilot, who unbuckled his parachute harness and fell to his death in the waters below. Having been shot down so far out to sea, it appears that the IJNAF pilots had chosen a quick death rather than perish from exposure or be mauled by sharks.

Pilots from VMF-112 with the squadron scoreboard showing 74 victories as of early June 1943. The majority of these successes had come during the defense of Henderson Field in the fall of 1942. (Tony Holmes Collection)

802nd Kokutai Sui-sen pilots pose for a group photograph on Faisi Island, in the Shortlands, in early November 1942. Hikotaicho Lt Toyoji Yamashita, wearing the pith helmet and devoid of flying gear, is seated in the middle row. By December the unit had been reduced in strength to just two serviceable Sui-sen. (Author's Collection)

Following combat with the Sui-sen, Foss attacked another "Pete," whose rear gunner not only hit his engine and radio but caused the high-scoring ace to duck as return fire shattered his upper canopy, barely missing his head. Foss decided it prudent to head home when his engine started to lose power, but without a functioning radio he could not communicate his predicament to his comrades. Heading south-southeast in the direction of Guadalcanal, his Wildcat was soon immersed in rain. All alone and hampered by deteriorating visibility, Foss soon became disorientated and unsure of his position.

Spotting a suitable island which he judged to be a good location near where to ditch, he set his fighter down in the water as close to the beach as he could manage. Following a relatively clean ditching, Foss finally made it to the surface after freeing himself from the cockpit of his submerged fighter. He then struggled to reach the island in his life vest, the floundering swim in the swell and current lasting four to five hours before he made landfall. Just after sunset, and completely exhausted, Foss heard splashing oars in the distance. Upon hearing someone speaking in English, he knew rescue was close. Foss had in fact ditched offshore a small island proximate to the large island of Malaita, where Catholic missionaries provided shelter and fed the exhausted aviator. Foss was returned to Henderson Field by PBY Catalina the following day.

In return for the loss of six Sui-sen, this operation had cost the Cactus Air Force four F4F-4s, with VMF-121 pilot 2Lt Cecil Doyle being killed. Aside from Foss, 2Lts Jacob Stubb and John Maas had also ditched and were later rescued. The crew of a VMSB-141 SBD-3 was also lost. These losses showed that although the Sui-sen force had ultimately been wiped out, its pilots had managed to regroup sufficiently after the initial attack to inflict substantial damage on the Wildcats. Nonetheless, the loss of six Sui-sen constituted a hard blow for R-Area Force, which was now almost devoid of floatplane fighters.

This situation was made worse with the departure of experienced Sui-sen pilot Ens Gi'ichi Minami the following day (November 8) due to tropical illness. Similarly,

A VMF-121 Wildcat is prepared for flight at Henderson Field in late 1942. This unit almost certainly shot down more Sui-sen than any other F4F-4 squadron in the Solomons. (Author's Collection)

*Kamikawa Maru* had lost Superior Airman Ryozo Kuwashima at the end of October when he too was sent back to Japan with a tropical disease. By mid-November 1942, the operational career of *Kamikawa Maru*'s Sui-sen had all but ended. Two months of frontline service had seen Lt Ono Jiro's promising A6M2-N detachment lose nine pilots.

The costly mission of November 7 had reduced 802nd Kokutai to two Sui-sen for the forthcoming month. Only FPO1c Eiji Matsuyama and recently arrived Superior Flyer Shinkichi Oshima continued to undertake missions mainly from the Shortlands, at one stage patrolling as far as the new airfield being built at Munda. During this time they rarely encountered enemy aircraft, although on November 15 over southern Bougainville they engaged eight Australia-based B-24D Liberators from the 90th BG.

The next action for Matsuyama and Oshima came just before noon on January 5, 1943 when they fought P-38s. Oshima was forced to bail out of his Sui-sen when it caught fire. Although he was soon rescued by a "Pete," 802nd Kokutai's fighter "force" now consisted of just a solitary A6M2-N.

By then, in Japan, the IJNAF was already in the process of sending urgently needed Sui-sen reinforcements to the South Seas. On December 17, Lt Cdr Tsunemaru Eto, previously *Kamikawa Maru* hikotaicho, was tasked with reforming a rejuvenated 802nd Kokutai at Yokosuka. The unit, allocated 15 brand new Sui-sen with the tail codes N1-101 to -115, consisted of 16 replacement pilots led by buntaicho Lt(jg) Takeo Yokoyama. The detachment sailed from Yokosuka on January 2, 1943 aboard *Kunikawa Maru* with six new Sui-sen, as well as 12 new F1M2 "Petes" destined for 958th Kokutai. The remaining nine Sui-sen followed separately, split into separate shipments between several merchantmen. Buntaicho

This Sui-sen was one of 15 new airframes assigned to 802nd Kokutai in December 1942 and then shipped to the South Seas theater early the following month. It is seen here taxiing in at Kulitanai Bay, in the Shortlands, following the rejuvenated unit's arrival in the Solomons. (Tony Holmes Collection)

Yokoyama and his pilots were later delivered to Poporang Island from Rabaul by "Mavis" flying boat on January 15.

Meanwhile, FPO1c Eiji Matsuyama had kept flying the lone 802nd Kokutai Sui-sen in-theater on solo outings until *Kunikawa Maru* offloaded replenishment airframes offshore Poporang Island on January 14. The six crated Sui-sen strapped to the tender's deck were soon flight-tested, bolstered by separate deliveries totaling nine more Sui-sen over the next few weeks. By January 18, 802nd Kokutai had nine airworthy Sui-sen ready to participate in Operation *Ke* – the highly successful evacuation of Japanese personnel from Guadalcanal that ran from January 14 to February 8.

At this juncture, an odd incident befell the new arrivals. During the afternoon of January 18, while the final batch of Sui-sen was being engine-tested at Poporang Island, buntaicho Lt(jg) Takeo Yokoyama scheduled a series of familiarization and training flights for his pilots, with the focus being on air-to-air gunnery. Using all nine Sui-sen at his disposal, each shotaicho (flight leader) took it in turns to tow a target windsock for his two wingmen to fire at. These windsocks were an ad hoc construction and had no auto-release mechanism, meaning each towing Sui-sen had to land to either adjust or detach the windsock.

The first practice shotai departed at 1405 hrs, just as eight Flying Fortresses from the 5th BG approached nearby Tonolei Harbor, escorted by seven Warhawks from the 68th FS and six Lightnings from the 339th FS. A flight of three P-40s was the first to encounter the Sui-sen of FPO2c Keiji Sunami with its windsock in tow. Wingman Superior Flyer Minoru Minasawa tried unsuccessfully to prevent the lead Warhawk from intercepting Sunami's sluggish Sui-sen, the floatplane bursting into fire and its pilot bailing out at low altitude – he was soon fished from the water by a

launch. The P-40 pilots then turned their attention to Minasawa, shooting down his Sui-sen. He too bailed out, only to be shot and killed as he descended in his parachute.

This action reflected what lay in store for the "new" 802nd Kokutai, which would encounter USAAF fighters far more frequently than F4F-4s of the US Marine Corps in the early months of 1943.

Now reduced to seven aircraft, 802nd Kokutai commenced sequential patrols in formations of six or seven fighters on January 19. At this juncture combat picked up to a relentless pace. On the 20th, Flying Fortresses from the 11th BG headed for Poporang Island just after dawn. At 0820 hrs, Lt(jg) Keizou Yamazaki led five Sui-sen aloft to intercept them, and shortly thereafter the floatplane fighters briefly engaged a quartet of 68th FS Warhawks before reaching the bomber. FCPO Shinji Ishida wounded Lt Frederick Ploetz, who returned to Guadalcanal with a shattered elbow. The Warhawk pilots in turn stated that they had been attacked by "Petes," two of which they claimed as shot down – none were in fact lost.

On the afternoon of February 2, the unit was tasked to cover the merchantman *Keiyo Maru* (with three replacement "Rufes" on board) and its corvette escort. Eleven Sui-sen launched from Poporang Island led by buntaicho Lt(jg) Keizou Yamazaki, who soon returned to base with a faltering engine. Lt(jg) Takeo Yokoyama took over, and despite standing instructions to stay together, the floatplanes scattered widely when attacked by three Warhawks from the 44th FS. The Sui-sen fired considerable ammunition in the action, during which seven P-38s from the 339th FS dived through them and shot down FPO2c Kiyoshi Akizuki. He too was rescued after bailing out, remarkably having sustained only light wounds.

An 802nd Kokutai Sui-sen taxies away from its moorings in the Shortland Islands in early 1943 armed with a single Type 99 50kg high-explosive bomb beneath each wing. Few primary records exist detailing just how well the A6M2-N faired as a fighter-bomber in the Solomons. (Author's Collection)

**PREVIOUS PAGES**

The final phase of Operation *Ke* (the evacuation of Guadalcanal in January–February 1943) marked the last time Sui-sen and Wildcats fought each other in sporadic but inconclusive aerial combat. Here, 802nd Kokutai shotaicho Lt(jg) Takeo Yokoyama, flying N1-112 from Poporang, briefly engages a Wildcat in a head-on pass off Guadalcanal in late January. From February 1943 onwards, with all Japanese forces having abandoned Guadalcanal, 802nd Kokutai switched its operational focus to patrolling over southern Bougainville. The unit would sortie between nine and 12 fighters for missions lasting from one to two hours. These patrols, designed to protect the Shortland Islands and the IJNAF airfields at Buin and on Ballale Island, resulted in numerous combats with American aircraft, but not with Wildcats, which lacked the range to venture that far from Guadalcanal.

Although 802nd Kokutai had lost yet another Sui-sen, the remaining aircraft assigned to the unit as replacements reached the Shortlands from Yokosuka shortly thereafter. Following the completion of Operation *Ke* on February 8, 802nd Kokutai resumed Sui-sen patrols over southern Bougainville, launching between nine to 12 floatplane fighters on sorties that lasted one to two hours.

## SUCCESSES

With the successful conclusion of Operation *Ke*, Japanese fighter efforts now turned to defending supply vessels and warships off southern Bougainville, as well as IJN/IJNAF bases at Buin, Ballale Island, and in the Shortland Islands. On February 13–14, land-based IJNAF Zero-sen fighters, supported by Sui-sen, succeeded in warding off American air attacks on vessels in the area, leading to a brief (but ultimately false) sense of triumph for the Japanese. As a direct result of this success, the remaining floatplane fighters were withdrawn from the South Seas after the IJNAF believed that they were no longer required in-theater.

On February 13, Japanese merchantmen and destroyers at anchor offshore Buin had been selected as a distant target. Two separate air strikes from Guadalcanal were planned, with the second to follow closely on the heels of the first. The logic behind mounting two attacks was that the defending Zero-sen would retire to refuel after the first strike, leaving aircraft in the second formation to hit their targets without any aerial opposition. US Navy PB4Y-1 Liberator bombers would conduct the first blow and USAAF B-24Ds the second.

Although American mission planners had recognized the threat posed to its bombers by locally based Zero-sen of 204th and 252nd Kokutai, they were unaware of the replenished contingent of Sui-sen in the Shortlands. Although the aerial engagements fought on February 13–14 involved no Wildcats, the Sui-sen nevertheless ably demonstrated its effectiveness against fighters of similar, if not superior, capability.

The first strike comprised nine VB-101 PB4Y Liberators escorted by 11 F4U Corsairs (a type that had just arrived in this theater) from VMF-124 and a quartet of Lightnings. After all of the Liberators' bombs fell wide of their targets, the aircraft headed for home with 12 A6M2s from nearby Buin-based 204th Kokutai in pursuit. The IJNAF fighters could not climb quickly enough to catch the retreating bombers, and neither could two formations of A6M2s from 252nd Kokutai. Crucially, however, aircraft from both fighter units were still airborne when the USAAF B-24Ds approached about an hour later.

In between the two attacks, hikotaicho Lt(jg) Takeo Yokoyama led 11 Sui-sen of 802nd Kokutai aloft from Poporang Island, 20 miles south of Buin, at 1220 hrs. The incoming second strike, which had initially comprised six B-24Ds from the 424th BS escorted by six Lightnings from the 339th FS and seven Warhawks from the 44th FS, would run into a force of 40 IJNAF fighters. Two P-38s and three Warhawks had aborted en route, leaving just eight USAAF fighters to protect the Liberators. Having fanned out ahead of the bombers at 14,000ft, they were soon engaged by 204th and 252nd Kokutai in a fierce aerial dogfight. One Liberator took a direct AA hit, while a second one was downed by fighters. Two Warhawks were also lost, one falling to a Zero-sen and the other to heavy AA fire. The four

Lightnings, badly outnumbered, now tried to protect the B-24Ds, losing one in the process. Although the USAAF fighter pilots were later awarded seven kills, only two Zero-sen were in fact lost.

The final American loss on February 13 was Capt Harold McNeese's unnamed Liberator positioned to the far right of the lead element at 14,000ft. Targeted by Zero-sen, the bomber's starboard wing was set on fire and its No. 1 engine knocked out. Shrapnel damage rendered the interphone inoperable, preventing the crew from communicating with each other. Both pilots grappled with the controls, the bomber "skidding" in flight after the outer engine had been "feathered."

It was as this point that the Sui-sen engaged the ailing Liberator, establishing a disciplined attack regime by flying alongside it out of range of the gunners. From this vantage point, each of them made individual passes, focusing on the bomber's nose. McNeese briefly considered trying to seek cover in cloud, but he discounted the idea due to the limited flight instrumentation (just the altimeter and airspeed indicator) left functioning after the fighter attacks. With instrument flying out of the question, he tried to outrun the Sui-sen by diving away. McNeese was soon flying above the waves, as he later recounted:

> We dove down to 100ft, just over the water at 270mph. We then flew NE across the NW end of Choisel, following the valleys and flying 50ft above the treetops. We were still being followed by about five or six Zeros [Sui-sen], but their passes were ineffective, as they were kept away by the top gunner. On the way across Choisel, the No. 3 engine ran away. Crew members believed we were flying across Warisi hills on NE shore of Choiseul.

US Navy F4F-4 Wildcats from VF-27 cruise offshore Guadalcanal in March 1943, around the same time Sui-sen were leaving the theater for good. Veterans of combat in North Africa as part of the Operation *Torch* landings in November 1942, the unit, then designated VGF-27, was embarked in the auxiliary aircraft carrier USS *Suwannee* (ACV-27) at the time. It arrived in the Solomons aboard the vessel in early January 1943, the unit being reclassified VF-27 the following month. The squadron was shore-based at Henderson Field from February to July 1943, but saw little aerial combat. (Author's Collection)

Three A6M2-Ns from 802nd Kokutai return from a mission. The pilot of the closest Sui-sen has just shut his engine down and is being guided to shore by the support crew. (Author's Collection)

Meanwhile, McNeese was wondering why there was no return gunfire from either the rear or side gunners. He asked his navigator to check out the crew in the rear fuselage. A flabbergasted navigator returned with the startling news that all four rear-positioned crewmen had disappeared. Furthermore, there was a gaping hole near the rear turret. It became clear that following the first fighter attack, the four missing crew had bailed out, believing the bomber's demise was imminent. It later transpired that after they had done so, a Warhawk pilot saw a descending crew member strafed by Zero-sen in his parachute.

As the Sui-sen continued to harass the bomber, several Lightnings and Warhawks tried to defend it. At this juncture, P-38 pilot Lt Robert Rist was shot down by Sui-sen just prior to the Liberator reaching the coastline of Choisel. Once over land, and following an extended pursuit, the last two Sui-sen finally turned for home. McNeese increased power on the two good engines then gingerly turned the bomber back toward the northern Choisel coastline for ditching. Unable to lower the flaps due to a lack of hydraulic pressure, he was forced to ditch "hot" into a moderate swell. Following a long survival saga, the gaunt crew were returned by a PBY to Henderson Field on March 4. The four crewmen who bailed out were never seen again.

Despite multiple combat claims by the bomber's remaining gunners during a 15-minute running battle with the Sui-sen, only the A6M2-Ns of FPO2c Katsushi Awata and FPO2c Shuji Furu'uchi had their main floats and pylons shattered by return fire. Both pilots were rescued by villagers in canoes after their Sui-sen sank upon landing offshore at their Shortlands base.

The combined ordnance expended by all 40 IJNAF fighters was recorded as exceeding 15,000 rounds of 7.7mm ammunition, and more than 3,500 20mm cannon shells, indicating the sheer scale of this action. Given the length of the engagement, it is clear that many of the Japanese pilots were forced to break off and return to base when they exhausted their ammunition. Overall, the USAAF had lost nine aircraft to the IJNAF's four (including the two battle-damaged Sui-sen that sank after landing).

A heavy bomber attack on vessels offshore Buin on February 14 was again opposed by South Seas Sui-sen (as well as Zero-sen), and the success the floatplane fighters enjoyed that day would further contribute to them being redeployed. This clash also saw the F4U Corsair in combat once again, the type being the de facto replacement for the F4F-4 Wildcat. The widespread and conclusive action which unfolded on that day during a repeat attack by PB4Y-1 Liberators would be dubbed the "Saint Valentine's Day Massacre" by the Americans due to the high number of US Marine Corps and USAAF aircraft lost. For the Sui-sen, the fight was a masterclass in cooperation between the floatplane fighter pilots and their land-based brethren flying A6M2s from nearby Buin.

The first clash occurred when ten 339th FS P-38 Lightnings, providing high cover for nine PB4Y-1s of VP-51, dove toward 13 climbing Zero-sen from 204th Kokutai. Eleven 802nd Kokutai Sui-sen, led by Lt(jg) Takeo Yokoyama, had also taken off when reports of an approaching formation reached the Shortlands. However, a single A6M2-N was soon forced to return when FPO1c Mikazu Hirana suffered problems with his engine. Aside from the 204th Kokutai aircraft, the Sui-sen joined 18 A6M2s from 252nd Kokutai that had scrambled from nearby Ballale airfield.

Having failed to stop the bomb run on six transports at anchor off Buin, the IJNAF fighters relentlessly pressed home their attacks against the departing Liberators. The first casualty was PB4Y-1 "51-P-3," which was hit in the cockpit during a head-on pass that drove it into the sea south of the Shortlands. The bomber had been targeted in a joint attack by both 204th Kokutai Zero-sen and 802nd Kokutai Sui-sen. The same fighters then turned their attention to PB4Y Liberator "51-P-4," which struggled back in the direction of Guadalcanal until its crew were forced to ditch 12 miles offshore New Georgia. There were no survivors from either bomber.

Aside from the downed Liberators, four Lightnings and two Corsairs were also destroyed, although one of the P-38 pilots was rescued – 1Lt John Mulvey ditched off the Russell Islands due to combat damage and excessive fuel use, and he was rescued the next day. The VMF-124 pilots killed were 1Lt Gordon Lyon and 2Lt Harold Stewart.

802nd Kokutai had commenced its assault at 1210 hrs, with some of the pilots fighting for more than 30 minutes. These engagements scattered the Sui-sen, with the first returning home at 1315 hrs and the last some 25 minutes later. Incredibly, not one floatplane fighter had been hit, reflecting both pilot skill and the nimbleness of the aircraft, as well as a sprinkling of good fortune.

Against 14 American combat claims, the only Japanese loss was in fact 252nd Kokutai pilot FPO2c Yoshio Yoshida, who collided with a Corsair. The February 14 operation had proven to be a fiasco for the attacking aircraft with nine lost – five Lightnings (an F-5A reconnaissance aircraft had been shot down over Buin four hours prior to the strike), two Corsairs, and two PB4Y Liberators. The debacle not only showcased IJNAF fighter tactics, but also underlined the potency of the Sui-sen in favourable combat conditions.

American losses were of a sufficient magnitude that it was decided to cease further daylight missions against the Bougainville area until fighter tactics could be reassessed. This meant that the Sui-sen based in the Shortlands now found that their defensive

802nd Kokutai Sui-sen shortly after they redeployed to Jaluit, in the Marshall Islands, having departed the Shortlands for the last time on March 13, 1943. The ferry journey was made via Kavieng, Truk, and Ponape over several days. Three of the eight Sui-sen in this photograph have the Nakajima-applied green camouflage, the foremost being N1-123, which has its engine running. (Tony Holmes Collection)

role had been diminished. On March 1, two weeks into this lull in air attacks against southern Bougainville, Lt Cdr Yoshijiro Suzuki was promoted to overall commander of 802nd Kokutai.

With additional Zero-sen being sent to southern Bougainville bases, and the termination of Operation *Ke*, 11th Air Fleet agreed to relinquish control of the Sui-sen detachment to the Central Pacific theater. On March 13, Cdr Suzuki redeployed 802nd Kokutai's fighter wing to Jaluit, in the Marshall Islands. An H6K4 "Mavis" guided the 13 remaining airworthy Sui-sen to their new, distant, destination via Kavieng, Truk and Ponape – a journey lasting several days. A6M2-Ns undertook their first patrol from Jaluit on March 23, but they would not encounter the Wildcat in this remote Pacific location. The last Sui-sen had left the South Seas for good.

# STATISTICS AND ANALYSIS

All Wildcat versus Sui-sen combat losses occurred during 1942, and so it is within this year that specific comparisons involving the two types are most valid. The fleeting intensity of aerial combat saw both sides greatly overclaim the number of aircraft they had shot down – a common occurrence throughout the South Pacific theater, and an exaggeration which grew larger in 1943.

Sui-sen losses disproportionately favored the Wildcat not only in quantity, but for the IJNAF also in the quality of aviators lost. Many of those killed in the early stages of the campaign were elite pilots, with chutaicho and shotaicho, in particular, being irreplaceable. The Wildcat pilots on Guadalcanal bore the brunt of the island's initial air defense burden, and most importantly prevented the IJNAF from establishing air superiority over Henderson Field. By the time the Japanese evacuation of Guadalcanal concluded on February 8, 1943, it was the aircrew of the IJNAF that were more fatigued.

Tactics to negate the Sui-sen's impressive maneuverability saw Wildcat pilots adopt the "hit and run" attack – a well-placed quick burst followed by an accelerated winding dive to escape any ensuing attention from the fighter just engaged. The Sui-sen was unable to match the Wildcat in a dive, incurring reduced aileron response at high speed. As such, Sui-sen pilots found the tactic difficult to oppose.

The first ten A6M2-Ns lost in the South Seas were those strafed and destroyed by F4F-4 Wildcats on August 7, 1942, eight being moored in Halavo Bay and two more on the slipway at Tanambago Island. Nine of the ten Nakajima constructor's numbers were discernible from data and airframe stencils later salvaged from the airframes, the aircraft lost being 17, 739, 821, 822, 827, 912, 916, 917, and 919.

Adorned with three axe heads on its rudder to represent victories claimed in this aircraft by different pilots, A6M2-N N1-118 was one of only two Sui-sen of the original Yokohama Kokutai to survive the destruction wrought upon the unit at Tulagi on August 7, 1942. Transferred to the *Kamikawa Maru* air detachment on September 1, it was then passed on to 14th Kokutai the following month. Finally, on November 1, it was assigned to 802nd Kokutai. One of 13 "Rufes" sent to Jaluit in March 1943, N1-118 was the longest-serving Sui-sen to survive the South Pacific campaign. (Tony Holmes Collection)

The next batch of Sui-sen losses were four *Kamikawa Maru* aircraft shot down by Wildcats on September 14 near Henderson Field. Ten days later, another example was lost after being damaged by return fire from a B-17E, the floatplane fighter sinking shortly after it had alighted. Two more Sui-sen (tail codes YII-104 and YII-10) from *Kamikawa Maru* were shot down by Wildcats on October 10. Three days later, the first example from 14th Kokutai was lost to a B-17E that it was trying to shoot down. Two more from the same unit were lost on October 17 and 19, the first to a landing accident and the second to another B-17E attack. Finally, on November 7, a total of six Sui-sen were lost – five from 802nd Kokutai and one from *Kamikawa Maru* – in combat with Wildcats and P-39 Airacobras.

A straight comparison of loss ratios in combat for the Sui-sen versus the F4F-4 cannot be conclusive due to the limited number of engagements between the two types. Furthermore, nearly all of the actions involving the "Rufe" and the Wildcat also included other types of floatplanes and/or US fighters.

Arguably the most conclusive appraisal arises from the November 7, 1942 combat near Vangunu Island. Aside from Sui-sen and Wildcats, three other aircraft types were also present during this encounter in the form of the F1M2 "Pete" floatplane, P-39 Airacobra, and SBD Dauntless. Six Sui-sen were shot down, in return for the loss of four F4F-4s and one SBD-3. While these results are definitive, trying to sort out who shot who is less so.

The initial engagement with the Sui-sen was effectively a high-altitude ambush by the Wildcats. It seems from a reading of the numerous contact reports that only two Sui-sen survived this opening pass, with the others subsequently downed in a series of scattered dogfights. Capt Joe Foss, one of the Wildcat pilots who ditched, reported that the bullets which hit him were fired from a "Pete's" rear gunner. The P-39 pilots made numerous claims against "floatplanes," but whether these were "Petes" or Sui-sen

Two destroyed Yokohama Kokutai Sui-sen (Nakajima constructor numbers 739 and 821) were shipped back to NAS Alameda, California, for intelligence analysis following the capture of Tulagi. (Tony Holmes Collection)

remains unclear. Aside from Foss, three other Wildcats were downed, but who effected these losses is also unclear.

A total of 29 Sui-sen were lost in the Solomons in 1942 – ten to the August 7 strafing attack and the remaining 19 in aerial combat and/or on operations. Of the 19, eight fell in aerial combat with F4F-4 Wildcats. From the commencement of operations in the Solomons in mid-October 1942 until its departure from the theater, 14th Kokutai (which became 802nd Kokutai on November 1) alone lost seven pilots in combat. Its highest scorer, and the highest scoring pilot in the South Seas theater, was FPO2c Hisao Jitou, credited with three kills.

The Wildcat and Sui-sen were completely different types of aircraft, each with a set of strengths and weaknesses. All that can be concluded with certainty is that if these advantages were able to be exploited then one type would prevail over the other. Such circumstances were sometimes dictated more by chance than planning and pilot skill. Either way, the contest of Wildcat versus Sui-sen in this remote theater remains a curious sideshow to the main contest of Wildcat versus Zero-sen which so defined the Guadalcanal campaign.

# AFTERMATH

From February 1943, the Chance Vought F4U Corsair progressively replaced the Wildcat in US Marine Corps service in the Solomons. However, US Navy Wildcats continued to see combat in the theater until around mid-1943, when the Grumman F6F Hellcat began to make its mark – the aircraft subsequently became the US Navy's principal carrier fighter for the remainder of the Pacific War.

In other theaters, the F4F-4 Wildcat operated from escort carriers to provide air support for amphibious landings in the Philippines and closer to Japan. The Eastern Aircraft Division built 4,437 FM-2 Wildcats for the US Navy, this variant having a more powerful engine, lighter weight, and a reduced armament of four 0.50-cal machine guns when compared with the F4F-4, giving it a superior performance.

Meanwhile, the largest single loss sustained by the Shortlands floatplane base occurred on March 29, 1943, shortly after the last Sui-sen had departed the theater. The raid on the facility was undertaken by Cactus Air Force fighters led by P-38 pilot Capt Tom Lanphier. Consisting of eight 70th FS Lightnings and eight VMF-124 Corsairs, the strike targeted many areas of the base, destroying seven "Petes" from the *Kamikawa Maru* and *Kunikawa Maru* air detachments. On April 15, 1943 the entirety of what remained of the depleted R-Area Force was amalgamated into 938th Kokutai. IJNAF floatplanes and flying boats continued to use Rekata Bay, which was not abandoned until the loss of New Georgia in late August 1943.

After Sui-sen left the South Seas for good, they continued service in other far-flung parts of the Pacific theater. Perhaps the type's remotest location was the small atoll of Greenwich Island, located between Truk and Rabaul. Eight 902nd Kokutai floatplane fighters deployed here in October 1943, using the atoll as a base from which to attack American heavy bombers. Greenwich Island had first been used by IJNAF floatplanes

A Sui-sen deployed for home defense duties in Japan in 1944, one of a handful of surviving A6M2-Ns being flown by the Sasebo, Kashima, and Otsu Kokutai from coastal bases on mainland Japan. (Author's Collection)

in January 1942 when E8N2 "Daves" and E13A1 "Jakes" from 17th Kokutai set up a forward post there.

Sui-sen were later pressed into homeland defense, and by mid-1944 they were being operated by the Sasebo, Kashima, and Otsu Kokutai from coastal bases on mainland Japan. The type's last documented encounter with Allied fighters unfolded on February 7, 1945 when two Sui-sen briefly engaged Hellcats near Tokyo. In September of that year, a single Sui-sen of 934th Kokutai was flown by the RAF from Surabaya, in the NEI, to Seletar, in Singapore, and then on to Tebrau, in what was then Malaya, where it was evaluated by the Allied Technical Air Intelligence Unit–

This A6M2-N was briefly flown by the French *Aéronavale* post-war, the floatplane fighter having originally been assigned to 934th Kokutai in Surabaya. The Sui-sen was acquired as a war prize by the RAF, who evaluated it and then passed the A6M2-N on to *Escadrille* 85. Flown to Cat Lai, in French Indochina, the aircraft was found to be in generally poor condition by then, and French groundcrew struggled to keep it airworthy. Indeed, the "Rufe" crashed near Rach Ba Sang during its first operational mission on February 19, 1946. (Tony Holmes Collection)

Sat on purpose-built Edo floats, the prototype F4F-3S Wild Catfish was photographed at around the time the floatplane fighter made its maiden flight on February 28, 1943. Inspired by the Sui-sen, the aircraft failed to make it into production due to the rapid advances made by the Allies in the Pacific theater. (Tony Holmes Collection)

South East Asia). The aircraft was eventually handed over to the French *Aéronavale*'s *Escadrille* 85, which briefly operated it, among other captured floatplanes, from Bien Hoa, in French Indochina (now Vietnam).

While Sui-sen were fighting in the South Seas, the need for a dedicated floatplane fighter became less relevant as Japan moved to the defensive. Kawanishi had continued to progress the N1K1 Kyofu, but ongoing technical challenges caused serious delays. By the time it entered production in July 1943, Japan was firmly on the defensive, with Rabaul on the precipice of being abandoned as a viable air base. The Kyofu did see limited service, mostly in Southeast Asia, where the type operated from Ambon and the Aru Islands, both in the NEI, Penang Island, in Malaya, and from Singapore. A handful were deployed during the Battle of Okinawa, and at war's end they were also used in limited numbers for homeland defense with the Sasebo and Otsu Kokutai.

Returning to the Sui-sen, early reports from Guadalcanal of aerial combat with the highly maneuverable "float Zero" reached Grumman in the late summer of 1942. A subsequent request for a floatplane fighter by the US Navy prompted the company to rapidly modify an F4F-3 with its fixed wings, a standard production aircraft being converted by Edo and readied for flight testing within three months. Edo designed unique floats for the aircraft, which was designated the F4F-3S Wild Catfish – the first example made its maiden flight on February 28, 1943. Edo assembled just over 100 hundred sets of floats to complete more airframes, but the fast-changing nature of the Pacific War rendered the concept redundant and the US Navy canceled the project.

The original Sui-sen base at Halavo Bay was used by the US Navy in 1943–44 following its capture, and by 1945 the much improved facility was home to Royal New Zealand Air Force (RNZAF) Catalina flying boats. Today, Halavo village is situated along the foreshore parallel to the beach where the Yokohama Kokutai used to moor its Sui-sen, while the former slipway used by the RNZAF Catalinas is now the village football and sports field.

# FURTHER READING

Unfortunately there is little published material on the history of the Sui-sen in the Pacific, although, fortunately, there is no shortage of historical narrative on the F4F-4 Wildcat at Guadalcanal. Thus, research for this Osprey volume is drawn mostly from primary Japanese sources, and also the author's private archival collection, bolstered by Allied records contained in the Australian War Memorial Research Collection. Scant reference only has been given to the relevant Senshi Sosho series, a secondary-source attended with a multiplicity of errors. Most useful has been BBKS Kokutai Kodochosho unit operations records referencing 14th Kokutai, Yokohama Kokutai, and 802nd Kokutai. Relevant senjinisshi and suiraisentai senjinisshi for *Chitose* and *Sanyo Maru* and *Sanuki Maru* also host details of combined Sui-sen movements. The report by No. 6 US Marine Corps Patrol pertaining to the final days of the men of the Yokohama Kokutai in the hills behind Tulagi is contained in NARA RG38 Fiche 778.

## BOOKS


Claringbould, Michael John, *Pacific Profiles, Volume Five – Japanese Navy Zero Fighters (land-based) New Guinea and the Solomons 1942–1944* (Avonmore Books, 2021)

Claringbould, Michael John, *Pacific Profiles, Volume Eight – IJN Floatplanes in the South Pacific 1942–1944* (Avonmore Books, 2022)

Claringbould, Michael and Ingman, Peter, *Solomons Air War Series, Volumes 1, 2, 3 and 4* (August–February 1942) (Avonmore Books, 2022)

Ewing, Steve, *Reaper Leader – The Life of Jimmy Flatley* (Naval Institute Press, 2002)

Foss, Joe and Donna Wild Foss, *A Proud American – The Autobiography of Joe Foss* (Pocket Books, 1992)

Frank, Richard, *Guadalcanal* (Random House, 1990)

Jersey, Stanley Coleman, *Hell's Islands – The Untold Story of Guadalcanal* (Texas A&M University Press, 2007)

Kusaka, Jinichi, *Diary of Vice Admiral Kusaka Jinichi* (hand-written – held privately)

Nakajima, Otaka, *The Pacific War as Viewed from Combined Fleet Operations Room* (held privately)

Sherrod, Robert, *History of Marine Corps Aviation in World War II* (Combat Forces Press, 1952)

Tillman, Barrett and Carl, Major-General Marion, USMC (Ret), *Pushing the Envelope – The Career of Fighter Ace and Test Pilot Marion Carl* (Naval Institute Press, 1994)


## WEBSITES

Pacificwrecks.com website contains technical data about Sui-sen losses of August 7, 1942

# INDEX

Page numbers in **bold** refer to illustrations and their captions.